THE UNPLUGGED ALPHA (2ND EDITION)

THE NO BULLSH*T GUIDE TO WINNING WITH LIFE & WOMEN

RICHARD COOPER

Edited by
STEVE FROM ACCOUNTING

Second Edition, 2023

ISBNS

- Digital eBook Edition: 9781777473358
- Paperback Edition: 9781777473341
- Hardback Edition: 9781777473303
- Audiobook Edition: 9781777473365

1818 Dundas Street East,

Suite 202, Whitby, Ontario, L1N 2L4

www.richcooper.ca

I dedicate this book to all the men around the world that never had a strong, masculine role model growing up to teach them about the cold, hard truth of modern women and the world we live in.

CONTENTS

MY UNPLUGGING

> "*Learn from the mistakes of others, you can't live long enough to make them all yourself.*"
> ~ *Eleanor Roosevelt*

When it came to making mistakes, 2011 to 2015 were terrible years for me. I'd barely survived a divorce, my award-winning business was almost in ruins, and my heart was in pieces from a terrible experience with a single-mom that I dated post-divorce.

I knew I'd hit rock-bottom when I was seriously contemplating suicide in 2011. I remember driving my truck on the highway and thinking to myself: "If I just nail it, take off my seat-belt, and slam into an overpass freeway concrete pillar, it'll all be over quickly."

I was living in what psychologists have referred to as a "Safe World Theory." A belief system that is a place of refuge, and it was completely shattered during these years. Towards the beginning of 2016 I had all the symptoms of Post-Traumatic Stress Disorder (or PTSD).

Something needed to change - and fast. But it wasn't the world, government, or women that needed to change. It was me. I needed to wake up and update my belief system because what I believed in, and was doing, clearly, wasn't working for me.

In December 2016, I started my recovery when I was at a prestigious men's retreat. I was talking to a friend over breakfast about life, and he recommended a book called 'The Rational Male' by Rollo Tomassi. It kick-started my path to clearer thinking and helped me unplug from comforting lies. I soon saw the uncomfortable truths about the world that we, as men, all-too-often struggle through.

It's a book that opens with the question "Why do my eyes hurt?" And the answer... "You've never used them before." The quote is taken from the movie 'The Matrix'. During this infamous scene, Morpheus offered two pills to Neo: One blue and another red.

The "Blue Pill" offers a viewpoint that is one of falsehood, security, and the blissful ignorance of illusion. The "Red Pill" perspective offers us men the knowledge, freedom, and the sometimes-painful truth of reality.

I had subscribed to the notion that good, virtuous, and strong will always prevail over all things bad, painful, and evil. However, severe blows to my belief system forced me to question that notion and adapt accordingly.

In 2011, I began the divorce process, a few years after my only child was born. I quickly experienced the gut-wrenching reality of how badly family law treats men in today's Western world. How family law, and a female-first primary social order, encourages women to behave horribly, and without remorse, towards the child's father.

On top of that, during the separation period, I was also forced to defend an attack on the company I founded ten years earlier. This attack by credit card issuers with massive legal teams, threatened to put us out of business by changing legislation that would financially strangle us.

After getting off a phone-call updating my business coach in 2011, I vividly remember closing the door to my office and turning away from the window (so my staff couldn't see me). I then put my face into the palm of my hands and began crying uncontrollably.

Only two years prior, I was on cloud nine. I had built a multi-million-dollar custom home, my business was thriving, I was married to a lawyer who I thought was my "soulmate," and I was the father to a healthy child. Within one year I'd paid off my mortgage, and then bought my dream car.

Suddenly, I felt like my world was burning down around me. Before the divorce, my family and close friends always relied on *me* for being their rock, for being unshakable. Feeling this way was *completely* unlike me.

I spent $60,000 on lobbyists and a year and a half of my life trying to save my business. I was in charge of 23 employees and we had thousands of customers. To make the business viable again, we had to pivot into an almost impractical direction, which put me in a position where I needed to become the lowest paid person in my company to make things work.

The final blow that led to my awakening came in 2015, after putting almost three years into a relationship with a single mother and her two young boys. I was betrayed in ways I couldn't fathom by a woman who I believed in, loved, and trusted. I put a massive amount of personal equity into a woman and her children. Only to be abused, lied to, and ultimately cheated on by her.

My *entire* world was an illusion, and it completely shattered my beliefs.

After that breakup, and for longer than I care to admit, I was re-experiencing the trauma through intrusive distressing recollections of the events, flashbacks, and nightmares. I routinely woke up at 3am and couldn't fall back asleep as my mind was subconsciously trying to reconcile what happened.

I started experiencing emotional numbness, and began avoiding places, people, and activities that reminded me of the trauma. I also had great difficulty concentrating and getting things done. These were all symptoms of PTSD.

Trauma is a normal reaction to abnormal events that

overwhelm a person's ability to adapt to life. Leaving you believing that you are powerless.

One thing that happens when you start to unplug is that your senses become heightened and more aware. You gain a new sense of clarity; things or events that may have fooled you before, become more obvious and you really begin to understand *why* certain events happened in your past. We refer to this process as "unplugging" and we do it by updating our old belief system.

While some men get angry when they unplug from beliefs that weren't serving them, it calmed me. I became aware. Events in my life that previously didn't add up, *finally* made sense and I wanted to see how far down the metaphorical rabbit hole I could go. I needed an outlet and somewhere to express the lessons I was learning about how to live life in today's world as a man.

Fortunately, as I already had a platform, an audience, and a test bed to get feedback on my theories, I dove right into making YouTube videos.

After becoming frustrated with my divorce, and the attacks on my business from competitors, on May 23rd 2014 I created a YouTube channel to marry up my two biggest passions in life: Entrepreneurship and fast cars. I made videos and uploaded them to YouTube and called the channel 'Entrepreneurs in Cars'. It started out showcasing my entrepreneurial friends in their success rides, then giving away business tips and lessons from the trenches as an entrepreneur.

But I soon ran out of friends with cool cars and stories to tell. That was when a regular viewer of my work said: "Do a video on the different types of women to avoid dating."

Well, I had just broken up with my single mother and had plenty of experience on what *not* to do in life, so I began sharing those stories and letting my wounds become my work.

Since I began talking about how men could become better, by adopting a "Red Pilled lens" to view the world, I've had over half a billion views on various video channels.

Questions soon flooded in from my viewers seeking clarity on areas in life they were stuck on. Mostly on dating, divorce, marriage, self-care, business, and money. I also took so many questions from people going through their own unplugging struggles that I started coaching them one-on-one. I began taking copious notes and making videos on the lessons that I learned.

This book is a collection of my own personal experiences, the feedback from my community, and the *thousands* of people I have coached through their personal problems.

Many men have called me "The father they never had." That, by navigating this world with the truth that unplugging from society's comforting lies offers, I've taught them how they could live a better and happier life that enabled them to fulfil their purpose. I believe that it's my style of dispensing these experiences and cold, hard truth bombs that has helped others connect the dots and see the world as it truly is.

However, I must warn you: Some of these stories and lessons may be inconvenient and many will likely shock you. Remember, the truth doesn't care about feelings, or political correctness.

Ultimately, men live in a difficult time today as we are living in a "feminine first" primary social order. Men must embrace their masculinity and completely surrender to the notion that, by employing masculine virtues, there is still a place for men to become the best version of themselves in today's world.

Comforting lies from society, culture, religion, the government, mainstream media, and Hollywood all sell better than the uncomfortable truth. Which is why I believe wholeheartedly that a man's *true* mental health and happiness begins with an ability to unplug and navigate through life seeing things as they truly are - not as we've been told they are.

To get the most out of this book, clear your head, and then really open your mind. Many of the concepts that I discuss will not be popular and some will be opposed. But, as I always tell my audience: "The truth will first piss you off, then it will set you free - if you let it."

Look, I am not university trained, with fancy pieces of paper with letters after my name, framed in mahogany on my wall. Like you, I'm just an ordinary guy that wanted to work on himself. A guy that can use a lot of key life experiences to point to some facts about life, self-care, women, money, masculinity, and navigating the sexual marketplace.

I truly hope you enjoy this book and the invaluable life lessons contained within.

Peace.

Richard Cooper

STEVE'S TESTIMONIAL (HIS UNPLUGGING)

66 **Note:** The book's editor "SteveFromAccounting" offered to share his experiences of what can be achieved if you follow my advice in this book and put in the work required to turn your life around and build that life you've always envisioned for you and your loved ones.

He still has a long way to go, but hopefully his Field Report notes at the end of nearly every chapter will help show you that you too *really can* achieve your goals in life - as long as you consistently adopt a positive mindset and put in the effort to do the work.

I was the poster-child for being a plugged-in Beta chump that was sleepwalking through life. I didn't own my shit and I was, to be completely frank, a fucking man-child for *far* too long. I prioritized my (now ex) wife's career over my own (traveling all around the UK for over 12-years while she trained to be a Doctor), I had *zero* concept of what a boundary was (and only very rarely had enough balls to stand up for certain things) and

I had let the years of childhood bullying completely decimate my self-worth as a person.

The chronology I created for my solicitor during my (less-than-amicable) divorce was *truly* embarrassing. I, quite literally, cringed when I read it back to myself. I was fucking *pathetic*.

It took a *substantial* amount of trauma to snap me out of my sleepwalking state. But, I now couldn't be anymore grateful to my ex-wife for subjecting me to it. However, it *definitely* took me a long time to get there. It **forced** me to take a good, long, and hard look at the shell of a man that I had become.

I then spent a solid 9-years diving deep down into the self-improvement/red pill rabbit holes. I've consumed *a lot* of content in this space. However, I can truly say that by paying attention to the content in this book and *actually doing the fucking work*, you too can turn your life around.

It's been a very long and arduous journey (with *plenty* of setbacks along the way), but I have already leveled-up every single area of my life where I'm in the best shape of my life at 44, I'm making more money than I've *ever* seen in my entire life, I've got a business that's taking off (accelerated massively by the advent of A.I.) and finally, I've come to experience what ***true*** genuine burning desire looks and feels like when multiple women **truly** trust my competence and leadership enough to *willingly* fall 100% into *my* frame.

And, holy shit, it's *such* a monumental night-and-day difference from what my marriage looked like, it still blows my mind. And the craziest thing? I'm only just getting started on this never-ending journey of living my best life for my kids and I.

Oh, and hypergamy is *awesome*. It helps you stand out *even more* in a sea of guys who don't know how it all works (like I didn't), or who do and are too lazy to be bothered to put the time and effort in.

Rich's insights pan out - they really, truly do. I've put them into practice since editing the book back in 2020 - and my results show me just how powerful his insights are and continue to be.

It's time to make it all work for you too. So, go take the content here that best connects with how *you* want to live *your* life (i.e. make yourself your own mental point of origin, with your own goals, passions, and objectives), put on your overalls, and go fucking **do.the.work**.

That incredible life you want can be yours - it just depends if you're prepared to put in the years of effort that's required to get it. Go make your future-self proud.

1

THE SEVEN SPOKES OF A HIGH VALUE MAN

Looks, Money, Status, Captivation, Frame, Unplugging, and Game

Sadly, when it comes to women, men aren't taught the importance of looks, money, status, captivation, frame, unplugging, and game.

Instead, men are taught that he must become less, so she can become more. To "Just be yourself," and that just being a "Nice Guy" is enough to attract high-quality women into your life.

Unfortunately, women don't work like this. They never have and they never will.

Women possess an evolved firmware that selects for the best-looking man they can get, who has sufficient resources, is competent, has a solid frame, isn't boring or a pushover, and has status. Not because they are picky gold diggers, or want it all, but because they need to ensure that they pass on the best genes and can retain access to sufficient resources for the survival of their offspring.

> *"Men view women as beauty objects; women view men as success objects."*

Most men do not understand what drives attraction in women, and the vast majority of men are getting terrible, or no results, with the women that they are attracted to.

This leads to frustration, resentment, and ultimately quitting. Women are born; men must be made.

Women expect men to develop useful skills, be masculine, strong, and acquire resources that a woman and her offspring can benefit from. Her sexual strategy is hypergamy and, as a result, it continuously asks her if you are the best she can do.

By this point, the quitters will protest and scream, "See! All she wants is your money, muscles, and when she is done, she will go fuck another guy and break your heart. This isn't worth my time!"

That's a loser's mindset.

There is a lot more to creating and maintaining genuine, burning desire from women. Truthfully, you should never level yourself up just to get women. You level yourself up to improve your life and create better options. Beautiful women should just be a natural byproduct of your hard work.

Most men behave like women are a scarce commodity, placing them high-up on a pedestal while worshiping them. Yet, nothing could be further from the truth. High value men who are maxed out and unplugged are scarce. Conversely, attractive women are everywhere. Don't believe me? Search the hashtag #fitnessgirl on Instagram, and there are millions of results, with the vast majority of them, objectively, being nines and tens (in terms of their looks).

Looks

How someone looks matters - there is no way around this. Based on their reported usage patterns, women's behavior on dating apps show that they find 80% of men unattractive.

She isn't basing this on what he does for a living, his bio, sense of humor, competency, how kind he is, skills, or even location. It's based almost entirely on his one main profile picture and, for the most part, men are horrible at projecting a strong masculine appearance with professional-grade photography.

When it comes to looks, women overwhelmingly prefer tall men, with high testosterone cues like muscles and a chiseled jawline. Given the choice, almost all women would rather fuck a bald and muscular 6'5" Dwayne Johnson, over a full head of hair 5'5" Tom Cruise.

However, with that being said, men need to learn how to max out their looks. Because, even with his height deficit, Tom Cruise still had an abundance of women in his life by maxing out in many other areas.

The first step, apart from not quitting, is to be at peace with yourself with what you can't change and max out what you can change.

A man that is 5'5" can't do much about his height. But studies show that 70% of a man's attractiveness is based on the appearance of upper body strength, with height and leanness accounting for only 10%.

When women are shown images of men's bodies in studies and asked to rate attractiveness, they subconsciously, but overwhelmingly, seek a 1.62 ratio of shoulder to hip width. Yet, most men in developed Western countries are fat.

You can accomplish a "V taper" along with a thin waist and visible abs at any height, by eating right and building broad shoulders, strong pecs, large traps, and a muscular back, by lifting right. This is an area that almost all men can max out in that will significantly improve their overall look.

Sadly, most men don't track something as basic as their weight, let alone their shoulder to waist ratio.

If you are out of shape and carry belly fat, then you **must** make self-care a priority. There is simply no excuse for being fat and out of shape. If you want an enjoyable experience with women and want to be spoiled for choice, then you must do the work to live in a strong, masculine, and healthy body.

Refine your style

Style is another area where men can improve looks dramatically. You should wear clothes that fit you well and complement your physique. Most men show they don't understand style, and are wearing clothes that don't fit properly.

In my early twenties, when I first worked in office spaces, I used to buy cheap off-the-rack dress shirts and suits and I looked terrible in clothes, but great naked. Most cheap clothing is loose and baggy on me because most of the population is fat - and that's how they manufacture it.

It wasn't until a girl I was dating suggested that I should get tailored shirts made that I started getting more looks and compliments from women. When I splurged and bought my first tailored suit, it was the icing on the cake and that girl I was dating at the time became exceptionally jealous of the attention that I was getting when we went to formal events.

I use this example to impress upon you the importance, and significance of, wearing clothes that fit properly. And how dramatically they can improve your looks - especially if you've put in the work for a nice physique.

You don't need to buy expensive tailored suits. Instead, keep an eye out for clothes marked "fitted" with a small percentage of the fabric blend from spandex to ensure a good fit. For more on style, read Tanner Guzy's excellent book 'The appearance of power'.

Hair plays a big role with looks, yet I constantly find men

with messy hair. Or worse, balding men holding desperately onto their disappearing strands of hair with bad haircuts. If you possess a thick, full head of hair, then steal a look. Find a popular Hollywood heartthrob, that has similar features to you, and get a good hair stylist to fix your hair to imitate that look.

Hair loss

When it comes to hair loss, you need to understand that the 25% of men with a hereditary predisposition to baldness start losing their hair by age 21. By age 35, 66% of men start experiencing hair loss, and by age 50, 85% of men display significantly thinner hair on their head. Even if you have good hair right now, chances are you won't as you get older.

Men spend way too much time and money looking for ways to hide, or slow down, their hair loss with prescription pills, lotions, laser helmets, micro needling, onion juice and the list goes on to hair transplants. Some of these can be somewhat effective for some men, but truthfully, all they do is delay the inevitable.

If you've a hereditary predisposition to hair loss, my advice is to surrender to it, because you are going to lose it. The gene usually skips a generation; my dad has his hair, his father did too, and so does my youngest brother. My grandfather on my mum's side, however, was bald. So, my middle brother and I are balding and got the short end of the genetic stick..

I started noticing signs of hair loss around the age of 21 when I would take my motorcycle helmet off and notice a half dozen strands of hair in the helmet, but I kept a full head of hair until my early thirties. By my mid-thirties, I was using clippers on level one because there was no hairstyle that could hide it. Once I hit my early forties, I finally started shaving my head.

Throughout my life, I've been losing my hair. Yet, I've never had a problem with women. I always had a look that they liked. I've learned that there is a good part of the female population that just loves the look of a masculine man with a shaved head. Dwayne Johnson, Vin Diesel, Bruce Willis, and Jason Statham are all balding men in Hollywood that have a look that women are not only drawn to, but in many cases prefer. Because they own it.

You will need to make sure you've got a masculine physique if you are balding, or bald. If you look fat or scrawny - and balding - it's a *really* bad image. No woman pines for characters in Hollywood that remind them of George Costanza from the sitcom 'Seinfeld.'

Surrender to it and adopt an image that suits your stage of hair loss. There is nothing on the market today - that I am aware of- that will truly reverse male pattern baldness permanently. There are band-aid solutions and are at best only mildly successful at slowing down hair loss, and some are so pathetic they aren't fooling anyone.

Picture perfect

There's a great misconception from quitters that will lead you to believe that you can't do anything about your looks, and that women only ever date handsome men. Yet, if you Google "Joe Manganiello transformation," you'll find a picture of a scrawny-looking high-school dork in bad glasses. A dork that transformed himself into a buff, handsome stud that landed a role as a male stripper in the movie 'Magic Mike.'

Lifting weights, eating right, improving your personal hygiene, and having a well-thought-out image can do wonders. It's called "looks maxing," and it's dressed in overalls, and looks like work, so most men avoid it. Therefore, making excuses to avoid doing said work becomes much easier.

The great equalizer in looks is photography. When it comes to pictures for dating apps or social media, definitely hire a photographer. I go into the weeds on this in the online dating chapter.

Surrender to what you can't control; max out on what you can.

Money

There's a prevailingly lazy notion that money is evil, and that there is only so much money moving around out there, and that it's in the offshore accounts of all the rich and greedy men. Not only is that a lie, it's also a loser's mindset.

You could steal all the money in the world from the most wealthy people, and redistribute it evenly amongst the world's population and, within five years, I believe, most of that money would be back in the pockets of the people you stole it from.

Money is, simply put, nothing more than a store of value. If you acquire it, then that's because you've added value to the lives of others. Elon Musk has acquired a massive amount of money because he added value by solving massive global issues.

Throughout history, women have always preferred men with money. Women love a man that can "make it rain."

Even with your style and physique locked down, your looks will only get you so far if you haven't got any money. You should work hard to be in the top 10% of income earners where you live. As you get older, the significance of wealth increases because, like it or not, your looks *will* decrease. Even ugly, short, fat, bald men can have sex with really hot women if they have enough status and money. It is the ultimate equalizer for physically unattractive men.

Now, while stable employment is still the primary objective of most men, a basic J.O.B. (or, Just Over Broke) isn't enough anymore for most men today.

Women are graduating with more degrees and earning more. But men aren't and today there are more women earning more money than any other time in history. And because hypergamy never seeks its own economic level, women always want to date up. So, it's wealthy men that get some of the best results with attractive women.

When women ask what you do for a living, she doesn't particularly care about the "what" part. She is merely trying to be polite and curious about your status. More importantly, what she's really trying to do is assess how much money you earn.

However, the status component of your source of income does have some relevance. For example, a man that owns his own plumbing company might earn 50% more than a junior lawyer in a law firm. But hypergamy isn't all about money, it's about "the best that she can do." And if her hypergamy thinks a lawyer is more valuable from a status perspective to her than a plumber when introducing her new boyfriend to her family at Thanksgiving, then the lawyer wins.

A rich man can turn a broke woman's life around. But you should understand that a rich woman won't give a broke man the time of day (unless he's seriously hot, and even then, it'd only be for short-term sex). To complicate female nature even further, women will consider a poor man in his twenties if he has ambition and a plan (because he has "potential"). However, they have truly little patience for a poor man in his forties with only ambition and a plan.

To have options in life you need a surplus of money. Yet, most men live paycheck to paycheck.

"Fuck you!" Money

Every man in the West should *ideally* aim to be a millionaire by the time they are 30, or 40 at the latest. This isn't to beg for pussy, or for female validation. It's for you. So, you can do what you want, when you want, and have the confidence to tell people to "Fuck off!" that you don't want to listen to. Which is an incredibly powerful position to be in - in any area of life.

Truthfully, if you live in the West, especially in big cities like New York, Berlin, Miami, London, LA, or Toronto, a net worth of a million dollars isn't *that* significant, you are just average (at best), especially if you are over 40. Real financial freedom occurs when your net worth reaches 10 million or more.

There's no escaping the fact that money creates freedom and options. Women are merely a byproduct and they should *never* be the main reason that you continue to chase excellence.

Entrepreneurship, C-suite jobs (CEO, CFO, etc.), high-end sales (jets, yachts), major influencers, actors, athletes, and professional designations (think Doctors, Lawyers, Pilots, etc.), are the main categories where you can find the top 10% of earners women find attractive. STEM (Science, Tech, Engineering and Maths) can also pay well, but women are rarely chasing Google Engineers (even if they can make $700k/year) because they often find many of those Engineers to be socially awkward.

My preference is entrepreneurship, because it can be the quickest path to wealth, with the most personal freedom. But, while being an entrepreneur certainly isn't for everyone, it can often take *years* to get the role of a CFO, a Doctor, Pilot, or Salesman that sells high-ticket items (such as real estate or yachts).

Therefore. the ROI on investing in yourself is *absolutely massive*, and in my view at least, is well worth the work.

The point I'm making is that a factory job might have been enough for your grandfather after he returned from the war and then married your grandmother. But in today's world, that's not going to lead to a higher level of self-actualization for most men and, truthfully, it's not enough for today's women.

Men today are working twice as hard for women that are half as good as your grandfather's generation. Inflation doesn't just affect the financial marketplace, it also affects the sexual marketplace.

I want to re-emphasize here that while the point of creating wealth isn't to get women, you will naturally have access to more and more attractive women by acquiring wealth and status. As an intelligent man of vision and purpose, you must set boundaries and ultimately decide what kind of access you will permit women to have to your money.

Status

For men, status is mostly a by-product of wealth and influence, and we touched upon this aspect briefly when I was discussing money. Women, on the other hand, can achieve status with a decent physique, one million thirsty beta Instagram followers, but still be broke.

Part of the evaluation process women go through, when their hypergamous hindbrain is evaluating if you are the best that she can do, is assessing your status and influence.

Throughout history, men of high status have always had abundant access to high-quality women. In many cases, influential men of high status had harems of women.

Men of status are so desirable and in demand, that most women would rather share such a man with other women, compared to being saddled with a faithful loser.

When women get with a 5'9" Dan Bilzerian, they are happy to share him, because he is a successful, wealthy alpha, with thirty three million plus followers on Instagram. The man has status and so has an unlimited supply of smoking hot women who are much younger than him, who are willingly waiting in line for a chance to fuck him, share him, be in one of his Instagram posts - and the real kicker is - many of these women have boyfriends too.

Status opens doors for you, gets you meetings with important people, preferential treatment, and yes, access to attractive women.

Even ugly men of status do well with women. Mick Jagger, the lead singer of the Rolling Stones, was never seen as a handsome man, in fact, many called him ugly. Yet, as a lead singer of a high status band, women didn't care about his looks because of his status. As legend has it, he once left a date with

Angelina Jolie no less, to have a one-night stand with Farrah Fawcett.

I use these extreme examples to impress upon you the importance of status, and Instagram is just one way of hundreds where high status can be signaled.

An average looking 21-year-old man, who has just started promoting fitness courses from his business, can signal high status by having a good Instagram following of 20,000. This allows him to garner the attention and praise of a few thousand people with every Instagram post as he goes about the business of promoting his products.

However, when it comes to signaling higher status, that won't work for a 45-year-old man. For him to have the same measure of status in a woman's hindbrain, he must show that he has acquired wealth and has a more seasoned reach and status.

Status can't be faked, it must be earned

When I'm with my girlfriend and a random guy approaches me who thanks me profusely for saving his life with my videos, it reminds her she is with a man of status.

I also show status with the Japanese chef that runs the small, high-end, sushi boutique restaurant that I frequent. When I call on the speakerphone to pick up an order, he always recognizes my voice before I mention my name, he calls me Mr. Cooper, and is very respectful. It's even more obvious when I visit the restaurant in person when I'm on a date to eat in, because I always get treated like a VIP.

When I'm at the gas station, with my girl in the passenger seat, filling up my supercar, and people approach me to ask about or compliment my car, I signal status.

Listen, you don't need to be a Rockstar, or a billionaire to have status. All you need to do is make money and have people show respect and admiration for you. You get to decide how you want to signal status, but the more status you have, the more doors that will open up for you and, ultimately, the better you will do with women.

Captivation

Being captivating is often overlooked by many, especially successful older men. I've done plenty of consults with men older than me that are divorced, wealthy, and in shape, but are as boring as watching paint dry. They should be dating beautiful, younger women, but they can't because they never developed any interesting hobbies and pursuits.

What's the point of chasing excellence, and making serious bank, if you do nothing interesting with your life? Yet, you'd be surprised just how many men don't have interesting hobbies and are *as boring as fuck* as a result.

I've learned that you can do *anything* to a woman - except bore her. When I was a young man, my dates consisted of dinner (if I had enough money) and a movie. Pretty standard and boring. When I pivoted to picking girls up on my motorcycle, providing thrills, and taking them to unique places, not only did my cost of the date go down to a few bucks in gas, and usually a coffee, but her interest in me went up *dramatically*.

Women want an experience!

Life is short and it ends for all of us. Pursue your hobbies and interests, then invite women to *come join you* in that experience. It doesn't matter how obscure they are - as long as they aren't boring.

I had a coaching client once that came off as boring on dates. However, when I asked him what he does for fun, he told me about his over-landing passion, which is essentially off-roading his Toyota truck. His eyes lit up and he became alive and passionate when talking about it and how exciting it was exploring new locations. I told him to tell his next date he was taking her on an off-road adventure to see the most incredible sunset, and to assign her the task of packing a small picnic for the day trip. That day trip turned into an overnight trip to watch the stars.

Again, you aren't chasing fake interests or adventures for the benefit of women; you have interests that you are already enjoying, all you are doing is inviting women to join you in the adventure.

Younger, and more beautiful women **enter your world**, you **do not** go into theirs.

Frame

Frame is everything. In every interaction in life, whether it's at your job, in business deals, with friends (and especially with women), one person *always* enters the other person's world, whilst adhering to the boundaries and/or rules placed on them. If you are employed at a company, then you are in your employer's frame (with the contract of employment defining the boundaries and rules).

If you want to get paid, then it is *them* who get to set the hours, the tasks, and what you can and can't do. Want to stay employed by them? Then *you* must remain within *their* frame.

In business deals, especially contract negotiations, there is always an element of frame. It's usually the person that needs the other person less that has the dominant frame in the interaction.

When you're unplugged, describing how you want to live your life (i.e. how it is framed) should be conveyed in an unapologetic and confident way, and those values should also be outlined from the beginning (which is especially true when it comes to dating and women).

For example, if you want to date multiple different women simultaneously, then simply let a woman know upfront (in a relaxed, nonchalant way) this is how *you* are going to live *your* life, and she then gets to decide whether or not she's cool with your invitation to accept those terms.

With women, if you want to live as an unplugged alpha and have a good experience with women, she should *always* be in your frame. The previous example that went from planning boring cookie-cutter dates to over-landing adventures, and giving her instructions to pack a picnic, is a great example of bringing her into your frame.

When a man goes into a woman's frame, he asks her what she wants to do for the date, at what time, and where she wants him to meet her. Toxic feminism has tried to convince women that men and women are the same, and should be equal (even when it comes to planning dates). It's not just women that believe this myth, men do too. Ultimately though, women *hate* it when a man enters her frame and they are actually *repulsed* by weak men that want them to lead.

However, a solid frame can't be faked; there's no "fake it 'til you make it" when it comes to frame. You **must** become accomplished, disciplined, cultured, and strong to successfully find a woman who'll willingly **want** to enter into your frame. Today's modern women **will** test your frame, and push back to see how you react to her challenges.

These "shit tests" (or "competency tests") are common and - if you have a rock-solid frame - should be **welcomed** as it's a woman's way of testing to see if your frame is real so she knows you are truly competent (versus just pretending to be).

If you can handle her testing your frame (in a firm, but playful way), then she *knows* you can handle life's other challenges with the same level of competency and experience. She can now feel relaxed enough to trust that you'll keep her safe, allowing her to fully embrace her feminine side. The differences in a woman who is firmly within your frame (versus a woman who clearly isn't) are beyond palpable.

However, you can't expect a woman to enter your frame, and be a complement to your life if you aren't leading. If you take her out for a drink, then *you* pick up the tab, *you* open the door for her, *you* walk on the outside of the sidewalk and keep her safe on the inside.

Frame is being a gentleman, but it's also about maintaining healthy masculine boundaries with a woman. Boundaries that extend long into the relationship. Because, if you do not maintain your frame, her shit tests, if failed, will eventually put you through "betatization through a thousand concessions" which is discussed in this book. And her respect for you and trust in you will rapidly begin to disappear.

If you are dating, and she has made an effort to claim you as her own, but states she has plans to go to Cancun for her girlfriend's birthday, a man with frame simply reminds her that: "I don't take girlfriends seriously that go away for girls trips when they have a boyfriend." A man without a solid frame will, more than likely, ignore his gut and will make the concession and let her go.

However, as an unplugged man, you can calmly state that you don't want to expose her, or what you are building within the relationship, to that risk. A man with a solid frame won't budge on his principles and will let her make her choice.

That means, if she decides to go against your frame and take the trip, then she has to collect any belongings she had at your place, and you move to replace her because she has demonstrated that she can't be led, or that she does not respect your healthy boundaries and values that preserve a good relationship and how you wish to live your life.

The Power of "I" vs "You" statements

One of the easiest ways of maintaining your frame (so you don't come across as "controlling", while achieving the same results) is to use "I" statements instead of "You" statements.

"I" statements convey standards, confidence, high values, non-neediness, that you are secure in yourself, and you have a healthy level of self-respect. Using "You" statements usually conveys the complete opposite.

Let's compare the following statements:

1. "I don't date women who smoke. I find it deeply unattractive and an immediate turn-off."
2. "You can't smoke around me, so you need to stop smoking."

In that example, the desired outcome is to be with a woman who's not smoking. However, using "I" statements sub-communicates that you have high standards/values and that she is welcome to continue smoking should she want to. However, *you* won't be giving her any further time and attention if *she* makes that choice (and that's the key: *She* feels like she gets to choose whether or not she wants to stop smoking and willingly enter your frame).

You can pretty much guess how she'd react in comparison if you used the "You" statement approach instead.

By using "I" statements, you get to define your frame in a healthy way for what you will (and won't) accept into your life. And, compared to using "You" statements, you get to do so in a way that communicates your boundaries in a substantially more positive manner.

Frame is everywhere, but easy once you know what it is. You will notice who's within whose frame when texting a woman. All you need to do is step back, read the thread aloud, and ask yourself "is she in my frame, or am I in hers?"

Society has sold us the lie that men and women are equal, and that we shouldn't call a woman we are with our "girlfriend" or "wife," they want you to call her your "partner." It's no wonder so many men struggle today with their frame (and then keeping her in your frame) when they have been told to treat her as an equal.

Men and women aren't equal, or the same. We are different, and should be a complement to one another's life, *if* the man's frame is the one leading in the relationship.

Unplugging

The unplugged man is a red-pilled man. He sees the story behind the story, asks questions, and doesn't blindly go along for the ride because they said so. The recent scamdemic of 2020 was a prime example of who was unplugged - and who wasn't.

The unplugged listened, but when it became clear that the scamdemic was nothing more than the common cold, and how they handled it was designed to control and manipulate us into a state of compliance, the unplugged stood on firm ground and resisted the masking, standing on dots, experimental vaccinations, and the shaming tactics used from the state officials, media, family and friends.

The truth of the matter is, most people are sheep and just go along to get along. That's a weak mindset that they can control.

Being unplugged means you won't be popular all of the time, but you *will* be respected. I have friends today that still don't hear from their family because they didn't take an experimental vaccine that ultimately proved to be neither safe nor effective.

Being unplugged means you choose freedom, options, and sovereignty over your life and decisions. It's no coincidence that most of the best unplugged men I know are libertarians that want big incompetent governments out of their lives and pockets.

The unplugged see right through woke narratives that they are trying to impose on our children like: rainbows, pronouns, trans ideas, inclusivity, and fat acceptance.

Remember when they demanded that we show a "health pass" to eat at a restaurant? But we can't ask what Rx medications Audrey Hale (the 2023 Nashville trans shooter) was on because that's a violation of human rights.

The unplugged ask these questions.

A very uncomfortable truth about the world we live in is that they have designed it to make us fat, sick, weak, incompetent, and reliant on group think, state leadership, and big pharma. They ultimately want to broadcast to us: "Jump!" and expect a "How high?" response.

When the unplugged learn that China bans what they call "sissy men" from the media, and wants to promote masculinity to boys, but Western countries do the exact opposite, they understand why.

However, just because we live in a clown world, it doesn't mean we must participate in their circus.

Game

Game is defined as you confidently using your attributes, characteristics, and overall personality to win the affection of women. It's about playing, and optimizing the cards you're dealt. It's also about turning your positives into swagger and your negatives into charm.

Game, when distilled, is about knowing what women naturally respond positively to.

Pick Up Artists (or PUAs) will tell you that game is the great equalizer when it comes to attracting women. If you haven't read the 2005 edition of 'The game' by Neil Strauss, then I strongly suggest you do. Neil isn't particularly good looking and wasn't rich at the time of writing the book, but the techniques he uses clearly proves that game works.

Game matters, but if you haven't got the other spokes to go with game, then you will only ever get so far with it. Even the legendary "Mystery" in Strauss' book ended up with a debilitating attachment to a woman because all he had was high-level game.

You can use game to get some success when cold approaching pretty women, while getting a number to set up a date. However, to be truly effective at game, then you must also be unplugged. Most PUAs have game, but not all PUAs are unplugged. Game without being unplugged is like owning a Ferrari, but without an engine.

To properly cover whilst being unplugged requires several books. Beyond Neil Strauss' book above, notable reads are:

1. 'The Rational Male' (books 1 & 2) by Rollo Tomassi, which covers the mindset and psychology behind .
2. 'The Mystery Method', by Mystery.
3. 'The Art of Seduction', by Robert Greene.

When it comes to these seven spokes, some will try to convince you there is an order of importance to these but, in my view, there isn't.

A man should do his best to max himself out in every area. One area is no more important than the other. A wheel isn't as strong or as capable if any of the spokes are missing.

They are synergistic and create a compounding effect as you improve in all areas. At the end of the day, the pursuit of excellence in these areas should be for yourself, *not* for the goal of getting women.

Women should only ever be a byproduct of you leveling-up your life in these key areas. As always, women should never be the focus of your life, only a complement to it.

The cold hard truth

Never forget:

- Men that do the work to put themselves into the most desirable top 20% have, by far, the greatest chances of sleeping with the vast majority of women. So, put a conscious effort into improving your physique, your style, and how you carry yourself. It'll pay dividends down the line.
- Frame is *everything*. It's how you define how you're

going to live your life and it's the boundaries that others must respect, adopt (and maintain) if *they* wish to join *you* on your incredible journey.

- Are you losing your hair? Who gives a fuck? Own that shit and make it work for you. Guess what? It's only a problem if you let it be one.
- Being wealthy affords you the financial security in life to tell people, or other opportunities, that aren't offering any value to you, to "Fuck Off." Money has an inherent value that allows you to pursue different options, or enjoy experiences that you previously could only have dreamed about before.
- Go make your own recognizable dent in the universe and positively elevate your status to "world-class level" in whatever field you specialize in.
- While you don't have to be an extrovert to be good at game (although that certainly doesn't hurt), you *do* need to build up a solid frame of genuine confidence that women can, quite literally, see you exude from across a crowded room. Are you having fun with women? Are you playfully teasing them and busting their, metaphorical, balls? Are you being your unapologetically authentic self around them? Are you only rewarding them with the value that your undivided attention brings because they've *earned* it? If not, then go and **Do. The. Work.**

Steve From Accounting's Field Report

It's been amazing to see how people in general (not just women) responded to me as I took steps to improve each of these areas in turn (post-divorce). Let's be clear here - I'm *definitely* no 6ft+ Chad with a full head of hair. I'm 5ft 6" and have a No. 1 buzz cut all over thanks to my receded hairline.

But none of that *actually* matters when you're out and about, truly living your best life because you are leveling up *every* area of your life.

And the differences between a woman who is **genuinely** within your frame - compared to one who isn't - are *absolutely mind-blowing*.

For example, I have a woman that I've been seeing casually for a year-and-a-half now. I never drive to see her - she *happily* drives 45-minutes twice a week to see me. She doesn't bitch at me when I ask her to bring drinks *that I like* (even if she prefers others), she willingly washes the dishes after I cook us a meal, and she doesn't complain that I'm still (discreetly and very safely) sleeping with other women.

I remember her asking me about smoking when I was driving us to a weekend away. We'd not long got into my car and she asked me if she could smoke (this was a couple of months in). Without skipping a beat I informed her that I don't want to spend my time with women who smoke, as I found it **very** unattractive and an immediate deal-breaker.

I remember she looked shocked and surprised, first at my directness and then my matter-of-factness as I responded. She then asked me what I'd do if she continued to smoke. Without skipping a beat I simply told her I'd "wish her all the best" and that I wouldn't spend anymore of my time with her.

She then got to decide whether or not spending time with a man that "ticks all of her boxes - and then some" was of greater value to her than smoking. Turns out, she values my time, attention, and sense of adventure more than she did smoking. And, she's *genuinely grateful* that she's in better health because of it. She also knows that if she **ever** smoked around me (or if I could tell that she began smoking again), that I'd end things on the spot. And she 100% believes I'd end it too.

She *happily* molds herself to fit within **MY** frame. "Shit tests" from her are now exceptionally rare (and are met with playful return and a passionate kiss that leaves her quietly stunned for a few seconds - shutting the test right down) and this allows things to become "effortless" (her own words, not mine).

When a woman trusts your - now more natural - ability to lead her **competently**, she feels *safe*. And when she truly feels safe, she will *willingly and happily* enter into your dominant frame.

And that's why maintaining my frame, values, and boundaries (in a healthy way) has been the foundation for some of the biggest improvements in my life - as a whole. Those things were non-existent in my failed marriage and my kids paid the price because of it.

I can assure you that if you take real, *meaningful* action in each of the areas covered in this chapter, that your life (as a whole) will improve *exponentially*. I've barely only scratched these surfaces myself and the results I've seen so far never ceases to amaze me.

The mere fact that you're actively doing the work to improve your life will - by default - make you stand out in a sea of simps, or of men who either don't see the value of chasing excellence, or who are just completely checked out of life and remain plugged in to society's comforting lies - like I too used to be.

2

MANAGE THE FUCKS YOU GIVE

When I was young, we played a lot of player-versus- player video games. There was a popular one called Mortal Kombat, and they all operated on the same concept. You started with 100% on your life bar and as you battled, each hit you took reduced your life until it was 0% and you'd die by some outrageous fatality resulting in massive carnage.

Life isn't much different. Essentially, it's about us taking hits all day long, draining our energy, attention, and resources until we hit zero. Unfortunately, most people don't value the energy they give away and they freely dispense it like it's an unlimited resource, and this is a **big** mistake.

Many people today see the barrage of hate I get for the truth I reveal in my videos, and they ask me how I handle it. Often my response is: "You need to learn to give zero fucks."

We all, by design, have a limited amount of energy that we can allocate to our daily lives. Everything we do takes time and resources. Our job, kids, friends, events, partners, and even the small things, like when my child wants me to kill a spider in the bathroom.

I refer to the energy that you can spend as the "fucks" you

can give. Therefore, it's incumbent upon you, as a man of vision and purpose, to manage every fuck wisely.

We are the masters of our lives, so we have the privilege of deciding where we want to dispense those limited amounts of fucks on. Only we get to choose what is truly fuckworthy in our lives.

When you drive to work and the asshole in the BMW cuts you off, you often choose to allocate those fucks to being frustrated. Rather than accepting it and saving those fucks for something else.

When a co-worker makes a disparaging comment because you won't donate $10 to "Donna in accounting's" fundraiser, you can dispense those fucks, and comment back with your feelings. Or, you can go about your business in a "zero fucks given" kind of way and ignore her underhanded comment.

To truly manage your fucks, you must first master self-control.

Self-control

You know that asshole in a BMW who doesn't signal and cuts you off? You have two choices:

1. Throw a tantrum in your car, wave your middle finger about, and flash your high beams, before accelerating up to his bumper - giving away some of your limited fucks in the process.
2. Utilize self-control, reserve your fucks for something more fuck worthy, and do nothing.

Option one burns up some of your limited fucks for the day and also applies stress to your body. Cortisol, a stress hormone, is released into your body when something gets under your skin, making it catabolic. Whereas option two does nothing. Ultimately, mastering self-control, and your emotions matters.

Those who are world class at their craft, and pursue

excellence, are *incredibly careful* about managing their time, energy, and resources. Ultimately, you can't become the best version of yourself if you're constantly re-allocating your energy to things which don't deserve that energy and don't bring you closer to your goals, passions, and dreams.

> "Where awareness goes, energy flows."
> - *Dandapani*

While this may seem like a simple notion, this idea was profound for me. I met Dandapani, a monk, at an entrepreneur's dinner event in Toronto where he was booked as the keynote speaker.

He sat there before us, legs crossed, on the floor, in full monk garb, with beads, and three white lines painted on his forehead.

He was an unlikely character to speak to entrepreneurs running successful multimillion-dollar businesses. They presented him to us as a Hindu priest with an Australian accent who had just finished 10-years in a monastery in Hawaii.

Entrepreneurs are notoriously prone to distractions, and many have varying degrees of Attention Deficit Disorder (or ADD). They are like herding cats. This monk was there to help entrepreneurs understand the notion of what "Energy Vampires" are, and how to manage their awareness to be more effective in their businesses.

Awareness, he explained, is like a glowing ball of light which moves around in your head, and when it goes to a particular area of the mind, then that area is lit up, which is where your energy flows.

So, if awareness goes to a happy area of the mind, then that is where your energy is flowing. And, if energy is flowing to the happy area of the mind, then it is also strengthening this area of the mind.

In order to manage your fucks, you must understand that

the biggest threat comes from people, places, or things which are "Energy Vampires." These are usually people that will take up your time, drain your energy, and leave you feeling exhausted from your encounter with them.

The keyword here is "exhausted" after your encounter. For more on that, search for 'How to deal with Energy Vampires' on my channel.

Mastering self-control

So how do you master self-control? Self-control is perhaps the most powerful skill you can develop that will help you master a better life.

When you learn how to manage your fucks and walk away from Energy Vampires, you exercise self-control, and start preserving your fucks for truly fuckworthy things that make you happy in life.

How do you know if something is fuckworthy? Simple. If the dispensing of the fuck helps make you, or your loved one's lives better, then it's usually worth dispensing precious fucks on.

Some might argue that this is a selfish or unkind way to navigate life. I propose that you re-evaluate how serious you are about managing your energy if this belief is violated by my statement above.

If the dispensing of said fuck drains you, or your loved ones, then it is probably better if you use self-control and preserve those fucks.

Let me give you a perfect example. I dated a single mother once, and one of her core passions was dinner parties. She would invite guests that were exhausting to be around.

My date had one friend that would berate, criticize, and judge everyone - including her husband. Her friend was a typical stay-at-home soccer mum, with teenage kids, who also had an exceedingly high opinion of herself.

However, she was nothing more than an obese middle-aged

woman expecting people to agree with her worldview. She was, in fact, an Energy Vampire. Meaning that being around her was an emotionally draining experience.

Simply put, there was no benefit to being in the same room as her. I knew that she set a terrible example of what an adult woman should be, I knew I didn't want to have my daughter around that energy.

After I received a second invite to attend another dinner party. I declined and, as you'd expect, declining the offer offended my girlfriend and she tried to create an argument out of it.

I simply didn't take part, thanked her for the invite, and ended the call. We didn't talk for a few days, and she called me after the dinner event to apologize and agreed that her friend was an Energy Vampire.

You see, when you exercise self-control, you manage your fucks better. When you become aware of who is an Energy Vampire in your life, you will be forced to make choices that may offend some people. Guess what? That's okay. A man that is on his purpose in life will inevitably rub some people the wrong way.

Remember, if you value your fucks as a limited resource, you will only dispense them for things that are truly fuckworthy.

How do you strengthen self-control?

It's my belief that self-control is like a muscle, the more you work it, the stronger it gets.

One of the simplest ways to strengthen that self-control muscle is to do things that are physically difficult or that challenge you. If you are looking for a task to improve your self-control, then taking a cold shower for most people is hard. Especially if you've had access to hot water all your life. Hot water is a modern luxury, but for millions of years we have been bathing in icy lakes and rivers.

To take a cold shower requires self-control. However, most people don't even have the ability to do something basic like stand in uncomfortably cold water in a shower. I urge you to start taking cold showers for the following reasons:

- It strengthens your self-control.
- It also offers the following health benefits: Reduced brain fog and improved focus.
- Improves circulation. Keeps skin & hair healthy. Strengthens immunity.
- Improves energy and wellbeing.
- Improves metabolism and fat burning abilities.

Do you want to improve your self-control and learn how to manage your fucks better? Then start by doing something as simple as taking cold showers. It's easy to understand, simple to execute on, but takes discipline and willpower to build.

I was speaking at a conference and closed off my talk speaking about managing your fucks, and someone asked me in the audience about how they felt anxiety over dispensing their fucks, and how to reserve them better.

The bottom line is this: If you value your fucks as a resource that has a limit to it, then you will only allocate your limited fucks towards matters that truly deserve your fucks.

The cold hard truth

Never forget:

- The energy that you begin every day with is extremely limited. So, stop wasting it on things that don't help drive you, your mission, or your family forwards in life.
- Giving a shit about every little thing that happens will only go to raise your cortisol levels. In turn, you get worked up over nothing important, while you

simultaneously tank your Testosterone levels. Be sure you've read my chapter 'Manage Your Endocrine System' for more information on this vital area of your well-being.

- There's also a good chance that if you go to bed with lower cortisol levels, then there's a much higher chance of having a far better night's sleep.

Steve From Accounting's Field Report

This one has *truly* had a profound impact on my life (and it also proved to be *invaluable* during my contentious divorce). Learning to let go of the things that were either out of my control, or that *truly* weren't worth worrying about (i.e "fuck worthy") meant that my life **immediately** became *far* more peaceful.

For a start, it allowed me to see past my ex's bullshit accusations during the divorce, ensuring that I only responded to key aspects that actually *required* a response, or my attention.

I went from never wanting to read any messages from my ex-wife while we were divorcing (due to the anxiety of wondering what BS she was going to come up with now), to truly giving zero fucks over the content of said messages. In fact, I usually have a genuine chuckle to myself as I can now see her blatant emotional outbursts for what they truly are.

I then employ the "yellow rock" communication method (*vital* if you have kids and are dealing with a high-conflict ex) and only reply, in a civil business-like manner, to what's *actually* important.

With my work, my stress levels have dropped *significantly* as I turned down projects that I know I simply didn't want to do, in favor of projects where I knew that I could add far more value.

It also proves to be extremely useful when it comes to dating. Being able to not get butthurt at a woman who's not interested in you, or has ghosted you will make dating **far** easier and more enjoyable. It also makes you more attractive to women as needy men are *really* unattractive (and it's a **very** common trait in men nowadays).

This is ultimately where your frame (and your boundaries for said frame) come into play. The stronger your frame is, the less likely any bullshit will get to impenetrate your boundaries. If every little thing starts fucking you off, then your frame isn't *anywhere near* are solid as it should be. Best go ask yourself why, and then go work on it some more until it is.

Just like with time, you've only got so much physical, mental, and emotional energy to go around. Guard that shit with the importance that it deserves. Your close family, friends, and the ones you love will truly thank you for it.

TESTOSTERONE AND HEALTH

> **Disclaimer:** *This book is not intended as a substitute for the medical advice of a licensed physician. The reader should regularly consult a licensed physician in matters relating to their health, particularly with respect to any symptoms that may require diagnosis or medical attention.*

The male endocrine system is an extraordinarily complex collection of hormone-producing glands that regulate metabolism, growth, development, tissue function, sexual function, reproduction, sleep, mood, and many other functions.

The primary hormone men should be aware of tracking as they age is their testosterone levels. Because, even in a healthy male, your levels **will** drop somewhere between 1-2% per year from the age of 30 onwards (and this is in a best-case scenario).

Andrew Huberman famously defined the importance of healthy Testosterone levels in men on the Joe Rogan podcast when he said "It makes effort feel good."

The decline of testosterone in men is known as

"andropause." Unlike a woman's menopause, which is an immediate decline in her optimal hormones. The process in men takes *decades* and, for many men, is hardly noticeable.

Declining testosterone levels is a genuine issue for men for a bunch of reasons. These include:

- Your lean muscle mass decreases,
- Body fat levels increases,
- Mental clarity decreases,
- Sexual function decreases,
- Bone density decreases,
- Energy decreases,
- And the risk of some diseases increases.

Optimal testosterone levels in men are directly connected to living an optimal life. And note the word "optimal", which *isn't* the same as "normal." Most doctors, if you ask them to test your testosterone levels, will call your levels normal - *if* within the bottom 10% of government guidelines. This isn't normal, and it absolutely isn't optimal.

It's my belief that men should track their levels starting at the age of 25, and then every subsequent year, and if your blood panels show the need for exogenous testosterone supplementation, then you can decide to either fix it naturally, or go the route of TRT.

Some men will try to shame you for using Testosterone Replacement Therapy (or TRT), but understand that they are just jealous because **you** will do better in life. Hate *never* comes from above, only from people beneath you. People never get jealous of losers.

Once you start treatment, you'll track it about 2-3 times a year under the supervision of a TRT clinic or doctor.

For me, it was around the age of 43 that I noticed the following symptoms:

- Low energy,
- Moodiness,
- An inability to focus,
- A lack of morning wood,
- A lower libido,
- Less strength,
- Muscle wasting,
- More body fat,
- And far less motivation.

I knew something was up, saw how TRT improved the lives of several of my friends, and then found a local doctor that specialized in TRT. When I ran my full blood panel, my levels, according to government tables, were within the "normal" ranges for my age. Thankfully, my doctor didn't treat numbers. Instead, he treated the symptoms I described above.

Optimal versus normal

Nobody wants to be "normal." As a man chasing excellence, you want to optimize every area of your life. A good TRT doctor will treat your *symptoms* to optimize you to the levels you had around the age of 30.

It's important to note that I am not talking about reaching the super physiological levels that a competitive bodybuilder aims for. Their exogenous testosterone dosages will be 4-10 times higher than what a TRT doctor will prescribe; abusing testosterone **will** eventually lead to health problems down the road.

Again, you are aiming for the optimal levels you had around the age of 30. Most TRT doctors will prescribe between 80 to 200 mg of testosterone per week and then adjust your dosage based on the results of your blood work. Everyone is different in how they respond to TRT, there is no one size fits all method, and good clinics understand this.

A full blood panel, in most places in the world, will cost you around $150 and is *well* worth the investment in your long-term health. A full blood panel will give you a factual baseline from which to begin your health optimization strategy from.

My TRT protocol

I'm currently prescribed 90mg of testosterone cypionate per week and 1000 IU of Human Chorionic Gonadotropin (or HCG) weekly.

My blood panels also revealed that I needed to attend to a few other minor areas, which my TRT doctor has been extremely helpful with. He recommended supplements that have had a noticeable impact on my overall health.

I **strongly** suggest doing this under the supervision of a licensed medical doctor that specializes in optimizing male hormones. Some men will try to save money, and do this themselves, and get their testosterone from an underground lab in Asia, or their "bro" from the gym. But you never really know what you are getting, it's potency, and you won't have a licensed doctor guiding you. To me, the cost savings simply aren't worth the risk.

I've already explained the merits of optimal testosterone. However, one downside of introducing exogenous testosterone into your body is that your own natural production shuts down once your body detects healthy levels again. That means your testicles will stop, or reduce, producing testosterone, and sperm.

Some men do fine with just testosterone supplementation. But I found that within four weeks of starting TRT treatment, I didn't like the contraction (or aching) of my testicles. Some brain fog returned, and my orgasms weren't quite as enjoyable since sperm production was reduced. So, my doctor added HCG to my protocol, and I felt like myself again after a couple of weeks.

Some men don't need HCG, but others seem to do better with HCG in their protocol, as we have Luteinizing Hormone receptors throughout our body. It keeps your testes full and functioning, pumping out your standard explosive loads. HCG is also useful if you want to maintain fertility to father children.

How to boost testosterone naturally

There are a lot of bogus products on the market that claim to boost testosterone, and always seem to cost a fortune, yet many do little to nothing.

There are two ways to optimize testosterone naturally. The first is to remove certain habits or compounds from your life. The second way is with some vitamins and supplements that help your body produce testosterone.

REDUCE STRESS

Stress increases cortisol, and cortisol has a heavy negative impact on your body's ability to optimize its endocrine system naturally. For most men, it's either stressful jobs, or the women in their lives creating the stress. Therefore, find ways to reduce, or remove, stress where possible.

Reduce screen time and blue light

Screens emit a blue light which disrupts our circadian rhythm and sleep patterns. Either wear blue light blocking glasses at night, or cut out screen time three hours before bed. Now use that time to read or do something else away from any screens so you can get a full night's sleep. Get 6-8 hours of restful sleep as your body repairs itself when sleeping - which includes testosterone production and other growth hormones. Your body *needs* to rest and recover more than you realize.

Remove processed foods

If the 2.4 million years of human history were broken down into 24-hrs on a clock, we've been eating meat for almost 24-hrs, wheat for six minutes, and processed foods for four seconds. Get your nutrition from a variety of greens and animal proteins. Studies have shown processed foods to disrupt your endocrine system, so avoid them wherever possible and stay away from extreme diets that restrict variety.

Reduce body fat

Men today are fatter than ever, and excess body fat negatively affects testosterone production, and compounds the problem further because excess fat supports the aromatase function in the body. That is, the natural conversion of testosterone to estrogen increases. The more body fat you have, the more testosterone you will convert into estrogen, and it's why you see so many obese men with visible breasts today. Aim to be around 12-15% body fat.

Add vitamin D3

People living north or south of the tropics cannot manufacture enough vitamin D from sunlight, and the problem worsens in the winter months with less sunlight. The government recommends 1000 IU a day of vitamin D, but that's too low for most people; I need about 5,000 to 7,000 IU a day to even get my blood labs to show optimal levels in the summer, and about 10,000 IU in the winter. Vitamin D is critical in many bodily functions, including testosterone production.

Vitamin D needs the help of fats or oils to be absorbed into the bloodstream, so any vitamin D spray that is oil-based works best. However, if you only have access to tablet forms of D3, take it *after* you have a meal. The oils from the food will help aid the breakdown of the D3 tablets into the bloodstream.

It's important to note that it's possible to take too much D3, leading to a state of toxicity. While this may require sustained dosages as high as 40,000 IU per day for some people, for others, it may require less. This is why I *strongly* recommend that you get your blood panel done so you have an accurate baseline level to work from.

One of the by-products of higher D3 levels in the blood is calcium. This excess calcium has a tendency to be deposited in the arteries, where it can build up and calcify. In turn, ultimately risking a blockage in the affected artery if left long enough, which could be fatal.

Therefore, if you plan on taking 5,000 IU a day (or more), then you **must** have a look at taking 200 **micrograms** of Vitamin K2 MK7 for every 5,000 IU of D3. The MK7 variant of K2 is the most effective at working alongside D3. K2-MK7 directs the additional calcium into your bones (where it's needed most), and away from your arteries. A dosage of around 100 micrograms of K2-MK7 per 2,500 IU of D3 is a sensible start.

 Editor's note: Based on where I live, I take 16,000 IU of D3 alongside 600 micrograms of K2 MK7 every day. And I get my blood panels done every 6-months so I can track how well I'm optimizing my levels. Suffice to say that, for me at least, there's been a *direct* correlation between my D3 levels and my Testosterone levels in *every* blood panel I've taken so far.

It's so important, I also give my young kids some apple flavored D3+K2 MK7 spray every morning. One spray totaling 800 IU for spring and summer, and two sprays totaling 1,600 IU during autumn and wintertime.

In short: Don't underestimate the importance of Vitamin D3 in naturally improving your T-levels.

Avoid Electromagnetic Fields (EMF)

Electromagnetic frequencies have been shown to disrupt the endocrine system, and mitochondria. These are emitted all around us, all day from our cell phone, tablets, and laptops. Try to minimize your exposure to microwave (cell signals), Wi-Fi, and Bluetooth as much as possible.

Put a timer on your Wi-Fi router power outlet to shut it off while you sleep and keep all electronics or screens out of your bedroom. If you use a laptop, it's often sitting right on top of your testes, so get an EMF blocking pad to eliminate exposure. Also keep your cell phone out of your pant pockets, or away from the body at all times.

Add the following supplements

The following vitamins are useful in helping the body optimize its own testosterone production: A, B, C, E, Zinc, and Boron. Studies have also proven that ginger extract and Ashwagandha naturally help improve your sleep.

The herb, Tongat Ali has been tested in many clinical trials touting its effectiveness in increasing testosterone. You can also find my supplements, including testosterone boosters at www.theunpluggedalpha.com

In conclusion

Testosterone is what makes us a man. It's why a healthy male has three times the upper body strength as a female, it's what makes us aggressive, and rise to life's challenges.

We have seen a dramatic decline in testosterone levels in men over the last 50-years, and the subsequent rise of weaker, softer, and more agreeable men in society.

Environmental estrogens in food, toiletries, drinks, and beers are being consumed in record numbers. Added to that, the constant bombardment of EMF on your body in large cities everywhere you go, terrible diets, inactivity, and people's addictions to their blue light screens. Combined together, it explains why we've seen the general weakening of the Western male.

Simply put, without healthy testosterone levels you will never operate at an optimal level as a man. Make monitoring your levels habitual. It will be a competitive advantage when navigating a world that is slowly making most men weaker, slower, and dumber.

The cold hard truth

Never forget:

- Testosterone doesn't just fuel your sex drive. It also governs many vital functions within your body. So, increasing it is **vital** to your own physical, mental, and emotional well-being.
- Do absolutely *everything* you can to optimize your testosterone levels naturally first. It might surprise you just how much you can raise them using just consistency and self-discipline.
- Your T-levels might come back within the "normal" range. But that range might only be normal if you're 60+ years of age. Remember, get a competent doctor to treat your *symptoms* (not your number).
- Therefore, not all doctors are created equal in this area. Do your homework and shop around for a doctor who has real experience in this field.
- Going onto TRT is a *lifelong* commitment as your body will stop making testosterone naturally as your T-levels increase.
- Check your medical insurance (if applicable to where you live) to see if it covers TRT. If not, you

must factor in the ongoing cost of private TRT treatment.

Steve From Accounting's Field Report

In the UK I use a website known as medichecks.com and order their "Advanced Well Man Blood Test." What I like most is the ability to track my progress across every area covered by the test and I can even have my bloods drawn, in seconds, by a nurse at a local private clinic nearby (minimizing the odds of doing it wrong by draining it out of your pricked finger).

As you can see in the image, my D3 levels closely follow my overall testosterone levels. I fully expect to - naturally - get my T-levels back up to the upper-end of the scale by the end of this year as I increase my workout intensity (which I had to reduce due to a herniated disc). I'll also make sure to take a blood test every six months (from this point on) so I can continue to monitor my progress, optimizing my micro and macro nutrients, making tweaks to my daily supplements, nutrition, and exercise/rest regime as required.

I've also noticed that my kids (especially my son) have benefited *greatly* as I continue to give them daily D3+K2 supplements (along with a good quality multivitamin). He's grown up to be one of the tallest in his class and he also recovers quickly from any injuries.

Pay close attention to your own T-levels and you'll find *many* other aspects of your life falling more naturally into place. I'll continue to find natural ways to optimize my own T-levels until it becomes better to go on to TRT (and, as I've had a vasectomy, I don't have to worry about becoming sterile).

4

MASTER VIOLENCE

Throughout our lives we've been lied to and have been told things like "Nothing good ever comes from violence," or that "Violence is the last refuge of the incompetent." These statements aren't particularly truthful, nor do they embrace the value of the capacity for violence.

Violence isn't always the answer. But it is a legitimate response in certain situations. Men have an obligation for the capacity to be violent and, if exercised, should be decisive and lethal.

Most men today can't be violent, or even understand why it's a skill that men should master. The narrative we've had crammed down our throats is "Be kind, be humble, and that love is the answer."

But, the truth is, society (and especially women) don't want meek and incompetent men. What women *want* is a **dangerous man that is civilized**.

Women's darkest fantasies were discovered when Google engineers studied the use of search engines and pornography. The top five searches were stories about Vampires, Werewolves, Billionaires, Surgeons, and Pirates. Films often show such characters walking quietly, while carrying a big stick.

Therefore, when search engine choices trump her social narrative, believe her choices.

A powerful defense is the best offense

I believe that you need to learn how to defend yourself, and your loved ones, should the need ever arise. It's an essential part of becoming the best version of yourself as a man.

Learn combat. There are plenty of facilities within 10-minutes of most urban areas that will teach different forms of Mixed Martial Arts (so MMA). These forms include: Boxing, Krav Maga, Brazilian Jiu Jitsu, Muay Thai, Kickboxing, Karate, and much more.

Memberships are around $150 per month, and most classes are 90-minutes in total. Half of the time is spent on cardio drills designed to simulate improved endurance in combat. The other half of the time is spent on core skills.

Joining a Dojo offers four major benefits:

1. The cardio drills are some of the most intense workouts you can do, and great for your body and conditioning.
2. You learn how to use violence in a focused and productive manner.
3. Your network is your net worth and people that train in combat, for the most part, are not losers, so your social circle will also improve.
4. You'll have your ass repeatedly handed to you by more experienced members. This is a good thing. It'll teach you how to pull yourself up and how to get your head back in the game. Both metaphorically and physically.

My dojo offers plenty of MMA classes, but my favorites are

boxing for the skills needed to be an effective striker, and Krav Maga for its effectiveness in self-defense. Krav is known for its lethality and efficiency of the responses to attacks, minimizing the damage to yourself while keeping you on your feet.

Krav Maga is so lethal, it's not used in MMA fights because many of the responses to attacks are illegal. It's also the gold standard in training for close combat for many Special Forces units around the world. If it's good enough for the Special Forces, then it's good enough for me.

Also, one of Krav's greatest assets is that it heavily encourages "situational awareness". The ability to "read a room" is a life-skill that can get you out of trouble before it even begins. Or, at the very least, give you sufficient warning that an attack is coming your way, giving you ample time to dodge or prepare a counter-maneuver.

If I am ever jumped by someone with a gun or a knife, or by multiple attackers, and I can't leave the threat area rapidly, I want the ability to respond with a highly trained, and proportionate, level of violence.

You may never need to use violence. But, if the need arises, it's a tool that you definitely want in your tool chest.

Test Yourself

Once you have acquired the skills to use combat, test yourself in combat. If you are boxing, and have sparred several times, have all the correct equipment and your coach says you are ready, then have your coach find you an opponent, and schedule a fight.

Three, two minute rounds are all you need to see what you are made of. Nothing is more humbling than an actual fight. My first fight was spring of 2023 and my coach put me up against a man two inches taller, 35 lbs heavier, and 20-years younger. Overcoming the fear of losing in combat to another man, who by every metric had an advantage, was one of my great accomplishments that year.

After all, what is the point of training if you never test your skills and get in the arena? You can't learn to swim on dry land.

For those interested in my result, I edged out my opponent and won that fight. Nothing feels better, I now understand why fighters get in the ring and put their jaws on the line.

How did I overcome the fear? I used it. I made it my bitch. I understood I trained properly for several years, was prepared, and deserved my win. I also brought three very important people to the fight that knew how hard I trained, and proved myself in front of them. A great book I relied on at this time is called "The Cus D'Amato Mind" by Reemus Boxing.

The cold hard truth

Never forget:

- It's incumbent on you to know how to protect yourself effectively. Doubly so if you have a family.
- You need to try several forms of MMAs to see which one resonates with you best.
- You must stick with whatever self-defense MMA that works for you. Be sure to put in the hours and watch as your skills and overall confidence grows.

Steve From Accounting's Field Report

This is one of the areas I know that I have yet to dive back into. I let a fractured wrist in 2019 (caused during my first ever Krav Maga lesson no-less) get the better of me mentally, and I *know* it's a kick-ass, no-nonsense way of master violence (with the added benefit of improving your situational awareness - allowing you to get both your loved ones, and yourself, out of a situation before it becomes dangerous).

I absolutely believe in the value offered by being able to protect yourself and your loved ones. Time for me to rectify that right now in fact.

OWN A MOTORCYCLE

It is my firm belief that, as a rite of passage, every man should own a motorcycle at one point in their life. As Jon Bon Jovi famously sang, "I'm a cowboy. On a steel horse, I ride. I'm wanted. Dead or alive."

Whether you're a hero or an outlaw (or, like the best among us, a bit of both), the motorcycle is the modern-day equivalent of the stallion. It is a rite of passage for every man to own one in his life.

During a bitterly cold and rainy spring day in early April, I got my motorcycle license at 18 on a single cylinder 125cc bike. Despite the miserable weather, it was one of the best days of my life. I remember being so cold and wet, we'd put our hands on the scalding hot air-cooled fins of the motor to keep our fingers from getting frostbite.

However, getting my motorcycle license was one of the best things I did as a teen. And, as a rite of passage, as I transitioned from a teen to a man.

The most important skill you learn from riding a motorcycle is situational awareness. You learn to keep your head on a swivel, and you are constantly scanning around you for potential threats. Just about everything else on the road is bigger than you - and can kill you. Being aware of your surroundings at all times is a skill that men need to apply to all areas of their life.

Let me explain. The first office I rented for one of my early businesses was on the top floor of an old century home in suburban Toronto. On the main floor there was a psychotherapist. She was a lumpy, old, fat, stuck up woman. Who would come up, stomp around, and complain once a week we were "making too much noise" for her practice located below us.

My office window looked out into the parking lot. And she always had a steady flow of patients coming in to treat whatever disaster was going on in their lives. I did, however, notice two glaringly obvious things:

1. Most of her patients were thirty-five-plus year-old women, showing up in expensive SUVs with permanent scowls on their faces. They had a look of emptiness, anger, and resentment as they marched into her office.
2. When men came, there wasn't a single arrival on a motorcycle. Not one.

With hundreds of visits per month, and over our three-year lease, I saw close to a thousand of her patient arrivals. However, I never once saw a single guy ride in on a motorcycle. Let that sink in for a moment.

Masculine therapy

A motorcycle is many things to a man: It's often a friend, a statement, an adrenaline rush, a toy, a place to fuck and, of course, transportation. Most importantly, there were many times as a young man that my bike was my therapist.

Shit day at work? Ride the bike.

Girlfriend fucks my best friend for redemption because she

resented a threesome we had with her girlfriend a year ago? Ride the bike.

Didn't get the promotion I wanted? Ride the bike. Roommates driving me nuts? Ride the bike.

You fire it up, go out, and reconcile whatever your issues are on the road.

Motorcycles require balance, strength, and dexterity. Cars don't. When you go around corners, you lean into the turn, and hang off the bike while your knee hangs mere millimeters from the asphalt. The toll you pay if you make a mistake is often much higher than that of a car. After all, a car is effectively surrounded by a metal cage - and bikes aren't.

Even with all of that, I bet if you hopped into a time machine and went back to a time when horseback was the main form of transport and asked a young man what he thought of his horse, he'd likely describe a fond attachment to it in a similar manner.

Men need masculine pursuits. Throughout history, sitting on a living, breathing, beast capable of incredible feats of power was something that men have wanted to tame. While a motorcycle isn't alive, most sport bikes have F1-like power to weight ratios, and it has an internal combustion engine, so it does breathe. After all, an engine is nothing more than an air pump.

Shared interests

Brotherhood is another perk of owning a motorcycle. The only form of transportation I've always got a head nod, or a hand wave from others, was when on a bike. Regardless of make, model, or style. Everyone is friendly to you when you're on a bike. There were plenty of places peppered throughout the city where motorcyclists would meet up for a coffee, have a chat, and then go for a rip together into the night.

I had been riding bikes for 12-years when a friend, I would ride with often, suddenly announced that his brother had died in a motorcycle accident when a car hit him on the highway. I noticed that others got hurt too, mostly because of careless drivers not paying close enough attention to motorcycles.

After four different sport bikes, two Katana 600s, a GSX-R750, and a ZX-7R, I decided that no matter how careful I was, my number would come up at some point, and so I took a sabbatical when I hit thirty.

I'd be lying however if I said that I didn't miss my bike, leaving me with a hole in my heart that needed to be filled.

So, I moved into fast convertibles, a 2003 BMW M3 in Imola Red, lowered on BBS LMs which, at face value, may seem like a 180-degree pivot. However, it was close enough to satisfy the open- air feeling while moving at speed.

It not only had the added safety of airbags, and a metal cage around me, but I could drive with like I was outside without a helmet, whilst listening to music. I can still remember the first day I got the car, I dropped the top, cranked up Mötley Crüe's 'Kickstart My Heart', and left for a rip.

In closing

Motorcycles are of incredible value to a young man. For less than $10,000 you can buy something that will out-accelerate, and often brake better than, any exotic car costing 20x as much. While still getting incredible fuel economy because of its small engine size.

The only things a car can do better than a bike are: Carry more cornering speeds (since there are larger contact patches on the tires), transport more people, and protect you better in an accident.

Women also love a man on a bike. I was constantly giving women rides on the back of my bike. Often, while at parties, my friend's girlfriends would harass me to take them for a spin right in front of their boyfriends. By the very nature of how you ride motorcycles, it forces intimacy.

Bikes attracted women like a moth to a flame. These

women would press their breasts into my back, while grabbing tightly to my lower waist, and sometimes grabbed my manhood when they got comfortable on the bike.

Trust me when I say, women crave adventure, variety, and fun. Dollar-for-dollar, nothing gets a woman more excited than to grab onto you tightly as you accelerate your bike into a wheelie. Remember, women in their teens or twenties are in their party years, they are looking for excitement. They aren't looking for men driving big SUVs.

Therefore, I strongly believe that every young man should own a bike at some point in their youth. Or, at the very least, a fast convertible.

However, I'm not done with motorcycles yet, I've merely just taken a break. Mid-engine exotic cars are my bikes - for now.

The cold hard truth

Never forget:

- Bikes offer you an unrivaled sense of freedom and escape from the trappings of everyday life.
- When you take a woman on a bike with you, every single receptor in her body is in hyper-drive as the addictive, and heady, cocktail of adrenaline and dopamine surges through her body. And she'll be associating that feeling - with you.
- If bikes really aren't your thing, then make sure you emulate the experience with a fast convertible that screams FUN! from every inch of it.

Charles' Field Report

Unless you fly an $80 million sixth-generation fighter jet, riding a motorcycle is the best video game a man can ever play. Your whole body is at stake, totally immersed in the environment. You can feel the wheel lift off as you throttle, body pulled forward in a ball of momentum; the wind caressing your face, your hair standing up when your knee gently scrapes the tarmac as you pass the apex, accelerating quickly out of a corner. There are no virtual substitutes for this experience.

Some of the finest hours in my life have been on a bike. The 3-hour ride from the ghost town of *Monticello UT* to *Hall's Crossing*, on a tank of gas that affords only a one-way trip, not knowing whether the ferry would, in fact, show up to take me across *Lake Powell* to my destination.

It was over 100 degrees heat, completely devoid of human or human artifacts except my lone Ducati. As I look across the desert horizon, thinking to myself "if I just ride past that, I will be able to see my destination, or something man-made," I would soon be there and looking over the next horizon, wondering the same thing, again and again as the void extended endlessly.

It was an *astounding* planets-cape like the desolate Tatooine you only see in sci-fi movies. Both bewildering and scary.

Oftentimes I wanted to stop the bike and take pictures of the massive cliff drops in their crimson glory. But I was too afraid, "What if the bike won't start?" Under that heat, I would turn into dry jerky and vulture feed within hours.

Or when I was riding through the black canyon of the *Gunnison* and a massive thunderstorm arrived. I had nowhere to hide but to push forward. Drops of rain the size of fists clashed against my helmet and gear, the wind blasted my bike from edge to edge on the narrow canyon road.

In that darkness, I can barely make out Junipers bending to the storm 5 ft in front of me, while pegmatite among the cliffs, polished over million years, echoed blinding thunder flashes at me.

On a bike, I remember the pastoral tranquility of *Lake Como*, the salty breeze of the *Adriatic Sea*, the insanity of *Bali's* traffic, the bullet ridden walls of the abandoned *Serbian* factories, the chaos and road rage throughout *Tel Aviv*, and the dozens, if not hundreds, of girls coming up to me for pictures and rides (always say no to them).

On a bike, you witness the world and its beauty. You learn to become more aware, perceptive. You also learn to become more aggressive and take the initiative, yet you also develop a defensive instinct. You have pride, but also humility.

HIRE SLOWLY, BUT FIRE QUICKLY

In 2003, I was working for Canada's largest collection agency where I was well into my fourth year of service as a manager to a team doing $2 Million in receivables. My staff were well trained and loyal, which meant our recovery rates were incredible.

Earlier that year, I had a new VP assigned to our group, a French-Canadian guy from a very rough background. I remember him telling us stories about his difficult childhood and how his father shot himself in the face.

He clashed with me from the get-go. He would publicly disrespect me in front of my staff, and make me run detailed reports, which he never looked at, for his own personal amusement.

After a few months of putting up with his disrespect, something snapped inside of me, and I let him know what I thought of him. This is where I learned the valuable lesson that people get hired for their skills, and resume, but get fired for fit.

Towards the end of the year, only three weeks after I moved into my first house with a big mortgage, a manager's salary needed to come off the books for corporate cost cutting.

Guess who was selected by my loving VP to go home? Me.

The initial burn of being handed that severance package hurt. However, this push inspired me to go create my own business which helped to settle consumer credit card debt, and I will be forever thankful for that.

It was about a decade later when I finally learned the lesson to hire slowly and fire quickly in my own business. You can use this idea with women in your life, employees, business partners, and even friends.

Take your time vetting people. Get to know them and study their behavior. The choices someone makes, and how they behave, should always trump what they tell you if there is a conflict between actions and words. I.e., Don't listen to what they say, watch what they do.

If your Spidey senses tingle, listen to your intuition. It knows something is up. Intuition is the little voice whispering in your ear, and it often only becomes a loud shout when it's too late and you are going to experience a train wreck.

My single mommy experience

Shortly after my divorce, I got involved with a single mom of two boys, and for the first few months it was great fun dating her. After a few short months, she started suggesting that I meet her boys. This was when my intuition started whispering to me, telling me it wasn't a good idea.

But... I ignored it.

Of course, my intuition only became a shout when her older son manufactured indignation. He started throwing a bad hissy fit during a vacation, yelling at me, being disrespectful, and calling me names, because I enforced a boundary with them, they didn't like eight months after I met them. Their mother sided with the bratty behavior, completely ignoring the blatant disrespect and the fact that I was right.

In hindsight, I should have limited my time in that relationship to just her and let it run its course. I never should have become involved with her kids. I should have also quickly fired her ass and ended the relationship with her at that point and then moved on. Instead, I let the torture drag on for nearly two more years. I also endured several similar incidents because I, again, ignored my intuition. It ended in a colossal train wreck for me with a severe case of "oneitis," when she cheated on me (after I tried to enforce boundaries with her kids again).

The business partner experience

Shortly after I took my severance package and went home, I partnered with a friend of mine I used to work with to offer debt relief services to consumers. He still had a job that paid him very well, so I was doing almost all of the work and he was taking half the money out of the business account every month.

I was working exceptionally hard to make it work; we were making about $30,000 a month for a business with only two staff, and no overhead, so it initially felt amazing.

That was until I realized that my partner had a drug problem - and was a control freak.

My intuition was telling me to get out. But, once again, I didn't listen. It wasn't until eight months later when it became a literal shout out in my head. And only when my business partner was screaming at me over my insistence for him to quit his job and join me full time. In a full-blown state of hysteria, he began yelling at me that he "never put me on the corporate books," and that I technically "don't exist" in the business.

Initially, it ended very badly. However, I quickly picked myself back up and with the help of my brother, formed what would become Canada's most successful debt settlement company.

Anytime I've gotten into trouble with women, employees, business partners, or anything else, it was because I didn't listen to my intuition and fire that person from my life quick enough.

With women, friends, employees, and business associates, always hire slowly and fire fast. You must be fastidious with your time, and who you allow into your inner circle.

The cold hard truth

Never forget:

- It's incumbent on you to take your time with the vetting period. The "honeymoon phase" can apply in other areas of life - not just in relationships.
- Be vigilant and observe if someone's actions match their words. Ignore what they say and watch what they do as words can be empty, while actions speak the truth.
- If you find that there's an inconsistency between their words and their actions, then you must be prepared to cut them out of your life as swiftly as possible.
- Make sure you've done your legal homework when it comes to business partners (or LTRs/Marriages), then execute that strategy with military precision and speed.
- And finally, listen to your gut. It's your brain telling you that things definitely aren't adding up.

Steve From Accounting's Field Report

This chapter's ethos of quickly cutting off relationships that don't serve you has been quite a revelation for me (as someone who was a complete "nice guy"). I've applied it to *both* my post-divorce dating life and also to a couple of business relationships as well.

Rather than try and force a particular relationship to work, I've ensured that if I spot any incongruences in someone's words versus their actions, then I check to make sure that we're still both on the same page or not. If not, I wish them all the best in life (with complete sincerity) and then I cut them loose. There's no need to be a dick to people (that usually only goes to bite you in the ass again at some point - Karma's a bitch, and payback usually comes with compounded interest).

If you value your time (which is the single most valuable commodity that *any* of us have), then it's incumbent **upon you** to see if the relationship is serving you.

When it comes to dating, it's **imperative** that you have a true abundance mindset for this to actually work. There's no "fake it 'til you make it" here I'm afraid.

Funnily enough (and not a word of a lie), just as I was in the middle of adding my field report into this chapter, I received a WhatsApp message from a 31-year-old woman I had a date with last week. She wanted clarity on what I was looking for, I told her straight that I wasn't looking for anything serious (also re-affirming that I don't offer exclusivity), and she said that she was looking for something exclusive.

I thanked her for her honesty, told her that this wasn't going to work for me, and wished her well on her search. No drama. She's freed up my time.

Respect yourself and respect your time - no-one else is going to do that for you.

THE FEMALE PRIMARY SOCIAL ORDER

One of the most difficult concepts guys struggle with today, is that men live in a "female first" social order.

It's important for men to understand how we, as a society, value the feminine over the masculine, and also why that is.

Until a man accepts this reality, and updates his core beliefs, he will forever struggle with the reality that unplugging from comforting lies brings.

The average man has been fed a steady diet of silly narratives his entire life, such as: "Women are oppressed," "The patriarchy is evil," "Masculinity is toxic," "All men are rapists," "Women are victims," and "Women get paid less than men for the same work."

In actuality, none of these narratives bear any close resemblance to the facts. This outrage is manufactured by a "female first" primary social order, with it originating from a toxic version of feminism that is no longer about equality. But rather, female dominance and male submission.

When you pay attention, you will notice an ongoing narrative that dismisses the plight of men, and even somehow makes women the victim of male disposability.

Hillary Clinton illustrated this eloquently when she said:

> *"Women have always been the primary victims of war. Women lose their husbands, their fathers, their sons in combat."*

So, men die in war, but - according to Hilary - it's *women* who are the most affected. As if to say that the, often painful, death of a soldier fighting for the freedom of western culture is simply insignificant.

Men, the disposable sex

Dr. Warren Farrell is a soft-spoken, educator, activist, and author on gender issues. He was the only man ever to be elected three times to the board of the National Organization for Women, which is a feminist organization, and spent much of his life advocating for feminism.

During his work advocating for women, a switch flipped in his head when he realized that women are, in fact, not the oppressed sex. Instead, women are the protected sex.

But, when we change the discussion, and talk about a female primary social order that's not being the victim of men, then it invites anger, disbelief, and ridicule as if to say: "How dare you suggest that women aren't victims and that men are treated with disposability!"

In his book, 'The Myth of Male Power', Dr. Farrell spills the beans on everything he learned through his experience as a male feminist, while also pointing to the cold, hard, and indisputable facts about the "female first" primary social order that we live in.

Although he had advocated for women for decades, his peers and critics called his observations of the facts he observed a "Promotion of misogyny."

One of the cold hard truths that men need to get used to, is that, whenever someone has a problem with facts, the problem isn't with the facts.

The truth is, any narrative that doesn't put the feminine

first today will be manipulated, so it is therefore seen as misogyny by default.

Some of interesting facts I discovered when consuming his work included:

- Men and women have similar mortality rates with prostate and breast cancer. Yet, six times more money is spent on researching breast cancer.
- 85% of homeless people in the US are men.
- Men get far longer prison sentences than women - for exactly the same crime.
- In divorce, men are more often left financially broken, with little - or sometimes no - access to his own children, while family law enriches the mother (at his expense no less).
- Men, by a wide margin, enter more dangerous professions by becoming: Roofers, Fire Fighters, Law Enforcement Officers, Miners, and Soldiers. A whopping 94% of all workplace injuries are men. Men also commute further, and work longer hours than women do. So, while men do often earn more, it's because men take on riskier, and therefore higher paying, roles. Often because they try to buy their way, to female approval and love.
- 24 of the Fortune 500 companies are led by female CEOs. So, the state of California, in an effort to equalize outcome (but without an equality of effort, or merit), passed a law in 2018 to force publicly traded companies to put more women on the boards of directors. Yet, there is no such push to get more women into coal mines, offshore drilling, or on garbage trucks.
- In situations where a parent is required to pay child support to the other parent, men are twice as likely as women to pay child support. Yet, unlike the disparaging term "Deadbeat dad," there is no

similar mainstream female equivalent. Perhaps "Deadbeat mom?"

- More than twice as many men are the victim of violent crimes compared to women (even when including rape), and men are also three times more likely to be murdered.
- Boys are taught in a female-centric school system, mostly by women.
- From the earliest grades, schools do a better job educating girls. Women now earn a majority of Associate, Bachelor, Masters, and Doctoral degrees, and their share of college degrees increases almost every year.
- In every TV sitcom and commercial, men are portrayed as bumbling beta idiots. Incapable of doing anything right and are the butt of all jokes, while women are praised and celebrated.

These facts show us that society puts far greater value, and importance, on the lives of women over men. If you live in the west, we are not in a patriarchy as toxic feminism wants us to believe, you live in a matriarchy. Our system is ruled by women, for women.

Society treats men as disposable and women as the protected sex.

That's okay, because we've always valued women over men. Let's just be honest about it, rather than pushing lies about women being the oppressed, while men are the oppressors.

War brides

Throughout history, men have always been disposable, while women were valued and protected. Go back 20,000 years ago. If a hostile warring empire conquered a neighboring nation, then all men of fighting age that weren't killed during the conflict, were either killed afterwards, or put in chains and enslaved.

Influential young boys were recruited into legions to fight for the conquerors. While women and girls were taken into the conquering army, preserved as war brides, because of their value in childbearing.

To put that dynamic into perspective today, it's one of the reasons why women have a far easier time getting over a breakup than men do. Women, as a function of adaptation, need to be able to adapt quickly and move from man-to-man easily if they were to survive.

It's part of a woman's hypergamous nature to always seek the best male that she could get. Warring tribe wins? Then the men in that tribe now become her best option for survival by default.

Men have always been disposable protectors. Women have always selected the best men for survival. Even if that meant becoming a war bride to a conquering army that killed off, or enslaved, their family.

"Toxic masculinity"

We live in a time where "Toxic masculinity" means that "All masculinity is toxic." This is especially true anytime a man commits a violent crime, or mass shooting.

In 2018, 19-year-old Nikolas Cruz took a gun, shot, and killed 17 people at his former high-school. He had his face painted all over the media, with headlines purporting that his actions were the result of "Toxic masculinity."

The media published the following headlines after the event:

> "How Gun Violence and Toxic Masculinity are Linked, In 8 Tweets"
> - *The Huffington Post*

66 "Toxic Masculinity Is Killing Us"
- *The Boston Globe*

66 "Guns don't kill people; men and boys kill people, experts say"
- *USA TODAY*

This was a boy brought into a world by an irresponsible single mother that allegedly drank alcohol during her pregnancy. Lynda and Roger Cruz adopted him as an infant. 17 months later, the Cruz family learned that Nikolas' biological mother gave birth to another baby boy, from a different father, who they also adopted. Roger died when Nikolas was four, leaving Nick and his half-brother to be raised by their now single, widowed adopted mother.

Boys raised in a single-mother household have disproportionately higher crime rates and mental health issues. 73% of adolescent murderers grew up without a father. 85% of adolescents with behavioral issues originate from fatherless homes, while 85% of youths in prisons grew up in fatherless homes. The truth of the matter is the vast majority of teenage gang activity, poor grades, suicides, teen pregnancies etc all originate from single mother households.

From reading the articles, you quickly learn that Nikolas was never taught discipline, determination, or resiliency. He was also a product of the 'participation trophy' generation where "Everyone's a winner!" by default. Therefore, never needing to learn how to deal with defeat in life or rejection by women.

As his belief system lacked any ability to deal with women, or rejection, when he was bullied in school, and then rejected by a girl he was fond of, it wasn't surprising that he defaulted to the feminine programming he grew up on. Ultimately, resulting in an outburst of anger and resentment, that lead to him going on to kill his school peers that rejected him.

Yet, when I searched the internet, I couldn't find one news

article about how boys like Nikolas need a father growing up. Or, how 26 of the last 27 school shooters came from fatherless homes.

With an increasing number of boys being raised by single mothers, the vast majority of teachers being female today, most boys have extraordinarily little influence from strong, virtuous male role models growing up.

> *Toxic masculinity isn't the problem - a lack of masculinity is.*

If you are going to unplug from the lies, you've got to learn to question societal narratives as a man; constantly ask yourself why men are being demonized and women are praised.

Extinct Rhinos

I would frequent many entrepreneurial learning events in Toronto when I was in Entrepreneurs Organization, and there was a South African I met at a dinner once who told us an interesting story about how Rhinos almost went extinct at the hands of Elephant poachers.

Apparently the mass harvesting of adult male tusks by poachers, almost eliminated bull elephants in a National Park he was responsible for in Africa. Elephants are apparently exceptionally intelligent, are hierarchical in their social ranking structures, and I'm told they even mourn their dead. However, without adult male elephants to keep the herd in check, young male elephants were charging and killing rhinos, apparently for entertainment.

When they got the poaching of bull elephants back under control, the rhino population rebounded as well. The importance of strong males in society and the animal kingdom cannot be understated. We know today that the vast majority of degenerate teen activity is the result of an absent father during childhood, so it's no surprise this translates to the animal kingdom too.

The way forward

The point of this chapter isn't to anger you. Rather, it's intended to expand the scope of your thinking as a man to the realities of the modern world we live in. And accepting the reality of where we stand is the first step in moving forward.

The cold hard truth

Never forget:

- Third-wave feminism isn't even close to being about "equality." Rather, it's about female dominance and male submission.
- Hypergamy is an evolutionary survival technique that ensures the female, and then her kids, are looked after by the strongest, most resourceful man.
- Society often sees men as the disposable sex. For example, the classic "Women and children first" approach on sinking ships (or other disasters).
- Men make up nearly all suicides (with many of them being because of failed past relationships - especially ones that involve his kids that he's no longer "allowed" to see).
- If you can't learn to accept this way of life, then you run the very real risk of taking the "Black Pill" and becoming exceptionally jaded against all women and pursuing any type of relationship with them (whether that is spinning plates, non-exclusive LTRs, or otherwise). You can prevent this from happening by updating your belief system with healthy adaptations and then learning how to maximize your benefits while minimizing the risks.

Steve From Accounting's Field Report

This is one of those things that you can't "unsee" once you've seen it. Whether that's at places of employment, on the news, or elsewhere, I've come to see the "women first" mentality all over.

It's also been interesting to see this narrative being challenged more openly (and recently) on various different YouTube channels. Granted, whilst there are the "drama focused" channels (such as "Fresh 'n Fit" and "Whatever", where they try and explain these facts to younger, more modern women), there's at least been *some* form of pushback in the public (which is at least *something* since the first edition of this book was released back in 2020).

For example, the sudden, meteoric rise of Andrew Tate has seen a *lot* of these topics getting discussed in more of the mainstream media, with many generating a lot of intense debate. At the very least, Andrew has put masculinity at the forefront of **many** more minds that it did before. And that can only be a good thing.

Unfortunately though, from my experience on the dating sites at least, the "strong, independent, 'boss bitch'" persona is very much alive and well.

The reality is, is that women don't tend to care about the facts that Rich laid out in this chapter. They only really care about how *they* feel (which, as we all know, can change in the blink of an eye).

I've found it *far* more beneficial to simply accept the natural solipsism of women, let them vent their emotionally-led hearts out, and then get back to leading the frame of my interactions with them.

There's no requirement to fight them on this (many YouTube channels prove this today). Simply focus on understanding, then accepting a woman's nature for what it is, and then navigate accordingly.

If those "boss bitch" women are still single when they're

older, or chose to settle in a deeply unsatisfying relationship that they're leading, then let that be *their* problem - not yours.

I'd rather spend my limited "fucks"/energy on leading warm, feminine women that *want* to be lead. Everything else is just noise.

WHEN "MEN GO THEIR OWN WAY" (MGTOW)

There is a growing movement of men choosing to check out from the sexual marketplace completely. This movement of Men Going Their Own Way is better known by its acronym "MGTOW."

While I may agree with many of the grievances MGTOWs have with women and the world we live in, I don't agree with their response.

Some MGTOWs limit their female interactions strictly to casual dating (even if she is someone who genuinely compliments them and adds real value to their life).

In other cases, men cannot compete in the sexual marketplace and seem to be involuntarily "Sent their own way." Such men become what's known as an involuntary celibate, or an "Incel."

The problem as they see it:

- Truthfully, I've lost track of the list of grievances MGTOWs have raised about women. However, here's a collection of the soundbites I've heard most often:
- "Hostile divorce laws towards men that strip men

of their wealth and access to their children, while simultaneously enriching the mother."

- "Women have become overly entitled and bratty." "If a guy like Brad Pitt can be taken to the cleaners in divorce law, what chance do I have?"
- "Women are constantly seeking validation and attention on social media."
- "Women are Machiavellian opportunists with the power of the state behind them, while simultaneously being incompetent children who are run by their emotions."
- "If marriage was a business contract, you'd tell the other guy to go fuck himself."
- "Women make bad voting choices, repeal the 19th, and take women's voting rights away."
- "Feminism is a supremacy and hatred movement against men."
- "Women can file a false domestic violence claim with no proof."
- "Women get to be promiscuous with impunity today." "Fear of paternity fraud and cuckoldry."
- "Fear of Sexually Transmitted Diseases (or STDs)." "Gynocentric laws in most Western countries favor women."
- "Fear of a lack of any loyalty to 'a good man'." "False '#metoo' allegations."

These are all part of the struggle of men today, and these grievances have legitimacy.

The dangers of "Red Pill Rage"

"Red Pill Rage" (aka: The Anger Phase), is one of the initial, and most dangerous, phases of "unplugging" there is as a man. Now, anger is a natural, and very legitimate, response to something that you believe to be an injustice. Therefore, it's perfectly acceptable to feel angry about something. In fact, anger can be a great motivational tool to get you to refocus your energy in the right places.

However, if you become stuck in this phase of being angry all the time, you start to run the real risk of becoming overly bitter at both women and the world around you. This bitterness will continue to eat away at you as you let your brain go down to those deep, dark, places in your mind that you didn't even realize existed.

Look, the world as you know it isn't based on the idealism of "fairness". It never has been, and it never will be. Society continues to feed you your "participation trophy," pat you on the back for coming in last, and will tell you that if you're just "nice" to everyone (especially to women), that it will "all work out in the end."

Granted, most MGTOWs understand this reality. However, they prefer to play the victim card and keep themselves to themselves. And that's their choice. Unfortunately, it's also a quitter's mindset. And, by definition, quitters never win.

If you're coming out of a shitty divorce, or similar, and you need to hit the reset button on your life. Then sure. By all means, take the time to recenter yourself and truly learn how to become your own mental point of origin. However, this should only ever be a very temporary step before you use your newfound knowledge of the world, and the sexual marketplace, to elevate your life to new untold heights of excellence and happiness.

Surrender to female nature

Do you get annoyed at the sea for being wet? Do you get irritated at the sun for being warm? Then why do you get so angry at women for doing what's been in their biological programming since homo sapiens began roaming the Earth?

Like it or not, females developed hypergamy as a means of

survival. If a woman picked the wrong man to pair and breed with, then it would spell certain doom for both her and her child. So, making sure that she was getting the "best that she could get," literally meant the difference between life and death for her and her kids.

And because hypergamy has been hard-wired into them, nothing has changed as the years have gone on.

Learning to accept it and then navigate it

When you finally get to the "acceptance" stage of how the world and the sexual marketplace works, you'll be in the perfect position to "flip the script" and use this knowledge to your advantage as you navigate your way through life.

It's almost like having a superpower where you can "see the code in the matrix" in real-time.

The "Black Pill" solution

The standard MGTOW "Black Pill" solution is: Just go your own way and avoid women completely. Or, at the very least, if you do allow women into your life, never live with a woman in a way where the state would automatically, and legally, view such cohabitation as a marriage.

There also seems to be an underlying belief by some MGTOWs that, if they convince enough men to "Go MGTOW," women will be magically forced to fall back in line and start to love all men for who they are.

Throughout history, women have always dismissed men they personally deemed weak or incompetent.

Women simply do not get involved with men they see as quitters.

> "Women don't care about your struggles; they wait at the finish line and fuck the winners."

A popular comment I've read in my videos is "DDD" or "Dudes, Dogs, and Dolls." Dudes, or men, are used for friendship, dogs for companionship (and affection), while sex dolls are to be used for sexual release.

This sounds an awful lot like the toxic narrative feminists sell women. That: "All they need is their girlfriends, cats, and vibrators."

Sex dolls and A.I.

The "adult-sized doll" solution amongst some MGTOW is to have sex with an inanimate doll. Do a quick Google search for "sex doll" and you'll see what I mean.

I found a post on Twitter from user @Masumi with a pinned tweet of a sex doll looking like a "perfect 10." It reads:

> "You know she doesn't love you, so stop pretending, dump her and buy a doll today. Always loyal, always there for you, 0% chance of a false rape allegation, STDs, divorce rape, pregnancy, she will never ask you for more. Credit options are available."

As a marketer myself, I'm impressed by the copy, but I'm *not* convinced that it's the best solution.

And in 2023, with the advent, large-scale adoption, and rapid advancement of A.I. and Large Language Models (such as the, now infamous, ChatGPT), lonely men are now turning to these new, and ever-evolving technologies to fill the feminine void that they refuse to seek out in real-life.

OnlyFans creators are now using A.I. to charge these lonely guys big bucks to "speak" with her digital A.I. avatar. And some of these creators are making *a lot* of money everyday using this technology (which is still only in its relative infancy).

Not only that, if you Google "MGTOW" there are over 3.5 million results. There are hundreds of YouTube channels dedicated to men talking about why women are not worth your time. Yet, many sex doll companies sponsor these channels and often end their arguments about how you should "Go MGTOW and get a doll".

Yes, feminism has destroyed the nuclear family. Women are more masculine these days, less agreeable, more interested in seeking attention and validation on social media, and in pursuing careers. Divorce rape is a real problem if you get married. A woman can allege rape with no proof (ruining a man's career), and this is possible because the world is built around a female primary social order.

The risks women pose to men is fairly high. However, the MGTOW narrative sounds like: "You are a victim; down with the gynocracy."

Which sounds an awful lot like the toxic feminist narrative used by women which seems to be: "You are a victim; down with the patriarchy."

The biggest distinction between MGTOWs and feminists is that MGTOWs say you should quit a game which is rigged against you. Whereas feminists screech loudly and organize protests to march on policy makers just to bend even more laws in their favor.

Both toxic feminists and MGTOWs appear to have the same end in mind - the isolation and segregation of the sexes.

Look, life has always been rigged against men. This isn't some golden era of the cards being stacked up against men which we've never seen before.

Did the 300 Spartans say it was a rigged game when the Persians invaded and quit? Did the British give up when Hitler began a massive air assault on the British Isles during the battle of Britain?

Last time I checked, nobody won anything by quitting.

You win by figuring out what you are up against, adapting, and then mastering the game. At the end of the day, every struggle a man must face in life comes with some risk attached.

Be careful of anyone selling you fear, or a victim mindset. A victim mindset is a loser's mindset.

The real MGTOWs

In my opinion, the real MGTOWs, are the men that quietly go about their life, without constantly pointing and sputtering at women, society, or at anyone else who lives their life differently to them. This was what I originally understood this movement to be about.

Rise of the Incel

There is a sub-group of men that call themselves MGTOW. Truthfully though, it's not by choice. Rather, they feel that they can't attract women and haven't done well with them in the past, so they are now an involuntarily celibate man.

The soundbites used by Incels online, usually sound something like this:

> *"Why don't girls like me? I mean, I'm literally a great guy, just because I'm not attractive, or don't have money doesn't mean I'm not a great catch."*

If you are short and skinny, be short with muscles and rich. If you are ugly, be ugly, muscular, and rich. Napoleon was only 5 foot 5 inches tall. And Mick Jagger is as ugly as they come. Yet, neither of these men had much trouble with women, or success in life, because they worked their asses off.

The saddest thing of all, is that at least 27 mass murders in North America alone have been attributed to men that have openly identified themselves as an Incel.

These men never learned how to handle rejection, learn from their experiences, or accept that they had some work to do on themselves. It was always the fault of others or society for their results in life. Sound familiar?

Self-professed Incel Alek Minassian, posted the following to Facebook shortly before he rented a van and went on a killing spree in Toronto:

Private (recruit) Minassian Infantry 00010, wishing to speak to Sergeant 4chan please C23249161. The Incel rebellion has already begun! We will overthrow all of the Chads and Stacy's! All hail the supreme gentleman Elliot Rodger.

Minassian drove his rented van over the curb onto sidewalks, killing 10 people and injured 16 more. His reference to "Chads and Stacys" is relevant because the frustration was that, as Incels, they can't compete with stronger, more alpha, males (Chads), or the women (Stacy's) that pine for the Chads.

You'd think men "Going their own way," would just unplug from society and live their own peaceful life. But, the Incel uprising has shown us that there is a dangerous subculture to MGTOW.

Better safe than sorry

MGTOWs will say that feminism has destroyed the social contract between men and women. It's hard to disagree with that observation.

But, if you search for channels on YouTube about MGTOW, you'll find pages upon pages of videos with narratives backing these claims up with, very well thought out, analytical breakdowns taking it further into a passive aggressive hate movement.

Ultimately, persuadable and frustrated men are the target of these recruitment videos.

I happened across a video once by a MGTOW explaining that avoiding marriage isn't enough anymore, that feminism had infiltrated civil law to the point that vindictive women could file domestic violence restraining orders in the US against a man they weren't living with. And, even though they weren't married, she could divorce rape him, all without proof, without his knowledge, and without a shred of evidence.

All women need to do is claim that you are violent, and the law will immediately side with them. Scary stuff, right?

By the end of such well-presented lectures, they'll have many men, incorrectly, believing that all women are demons.

While I don't disagree with the threat, it's the significance of the threat that I question.

Let's dig into the math used…

MGTOWs are great with stats. The content creator in this recruitment video provided numbers that suggested there are 900,000 domestic violence restraining orders filed every year in the USA. Asking how would you, as a man, like to be removed from your house, have your car taken away, and half your stuff gone based on allegations, not evidence?

Now, what if women filed those 900,000 restraining orders? While this is unlikely to be the case, for the sake of argument, let's assume all of them were.

There are now 325,000,000 people in the US. Of which men account for half.

That leaves us with 162,500,000 men and we know that about 40,000,000 of those men are under the age of 20.

So, we can assume that there are 122,500,000 men that might have been exposed to this potential threat with a woman. Remember, in this recruitment video, the man isn't living with anyone else and is only dating women on an exclusive basis.

That's 0.7% of the male population. Statistically insignificant. Let's put that into perspective.

According to data from the Centers for Disease Control and Prevention, the individual American driver's odds of dying as a result of an injury sustained in an automobile crash (which includes pedestrians, bicyclists, and motorcyclists involved in car crashes), comes out to around 1 in 77.

That works out to 1.29%. The vast majority of the

population can go through life without dying in a car accident. However, MGTOWs are telling men the threat is so great, that all men should now completely avoid half the population or, "just get a doll."

In conclusion

Personally, I don't care what you do with your time, or where you stick your dick. A prostitute, doll, your hand, or a hot woman. I'm not the Penis Police. What I *do* have a problem with though, is other men in need of help being misled by people so they can sell snake oil to them. Weaponizing them to hate how society is, before selling them silicone dolls to have sex with for $3,000, or pushing them towards the digital A.I. equivalent.

Granted, men have the burden of performance; women just need to show up and look pretty. But, MGTOWs appear to want men to stop playing a game that, truthfully, no man can ever fully check out of.

Unless you live in a cabin in the woods, with no connection to society, you will always be a cog in the wheels of the female primary social order.

Even MGTOWs that scratch their itch by using a sex doll are part of the feminine imperative. They likely work with women and probably also buy products and services facilitated by women. Hell, even their sex doll that "Looks like a perfect 10," keeps them tied to the feminine social.

The only proper solution is to:

- Do the work in life, so you become high value,
- Make yourself your own mental point of origin,
- Learn how to handle rejection like an adult,
- Always be the one responsible for the birth control,
- Learn how to spot dangerous personalities,
- And, finally, understand what drives attraction,

game, and how to limit your risk in a hostile sexual marketplace.

If you allow a woman into your life, then it's imperative that she is a complement to that life, not the focus. It's incumbent on you to stay on your purpose in life. Constantly chasing excellence with a genuine belief of outcome independence.

Look, disconnecting from women might be an interesting place to visit for a short while if you get divorced or have had your heart broken. But it's hardly a solution to living in a world where half of the population are women.

The cold hard truth

Never forget:

- Temporarily stepping out of the sexual marketplace is only valuable if you've just gotten out of a shitty divorce or relationship. Taking some time out to chase excellence and to "Level up in multiple areas in your life," will definitely pay off for you. Just make sure you're receptive to the increase in higher-quality women that make themselves known to you now you're a man of higher value.
- Remember, 80% of women want the time and attention of the top 20% of men. Chasing excellence will easily put you in the top 20%. What you do with your options when you get there... Well, that's entirely up to you. Have fun.
- "Black Pill" MGTOW thinking is very nihilistic and unhealthy for your mental and emotional state. Men and women can certainly complement each other in life. Not all women are men-hating third-wave feminists. But, you do need to know how to "Find the diamonds in the rough."

- Finally, hypergamy simply "is". Accept it, embrace it, flip the script, and start using hypergamy to your advantage.

Steve From Accounting's Field Report

It's scarily easy to become stuck in the "Red Pill Rage" part of unplugging. I was there myself for a few years or so. However, once I **finally** came to *truly* accept female nature for what it is (*naturally* hypergamous), then I found that I could actually start to *enjoy* the company and energy that a genuinely feminine woman brought into my life.

I could lament the fact that I'm 5ft 6" and effectively bald, and project a *really* negative energy that pretty much no-one would want to be around (male or female). Or, I can own that shit and constantly work on improving the areas that *are* within my control.

I therefore spent a solid 18-months on my own, squaring away my own shit after separating from my ex-wife. And I'm glad I did. It forced me to take a close look at where I had fucked up and it allowed me to do some fucking work before I went back out into the dating market. And it was absolutely worth every drop of blood, sweat, and tears.

I'm in the best shape of my life (and striving to get into even better shape), I dress *far* better than I did before, I'm genuinely **much** happier, I'm smiling *far* more often, and I have no issues engaging in conversation with women.

I remember recently attending a new Salsa class that was more advanced than what I was currently learning. I rolled with it, had a laugh, and found myself dancing with a very attractive woman who was around 5ft 10". I joked with her as I danced, I even fucked up a few new moves (and just had a laugh as I messed up), but by the end of my dance with her, she'd *pulled me* closer into her (damn fine) body, and then squeezed my hand as I moved on to the next woman to dance with (which just happened to be her sister!).

Women *only* want 6ft tall men with a full head of hair? Fuck off with that bullshit. I've only ever had ONE woman tell me she wouldn't date me because I was shorter than her. One. In two years of online dating.

Guess what? If *you* don't give a fuck - then neither will they.

I'll tell you now, if you're sorting out your shit and are truly living your best life, then you'll *naturally* give off an upbeat and positive energetic vibe that's like fucking catnip to women. Combine that with a rock solid frame and healthy boundaries (that you're 100% ready to enforce unapologetically) and you'll often find yourself with more options than you ever thought were possible.

And if you don't? Well, who gives a fuck? You're **genuinely** living your best life anyways. When you come to finally embrace female nature for *what it is* (and not what *you* want it to be), then your interactions with women will improve ten-fold. Immediately.

Embracing it has also allowed me to see things from my ex-wife's position. Sure, she made unforgivable and unforgettable choices (repeatedly), but I can at least understand *why* she felt the need to make those life-changing choices. And I sure as fuck won't ever make the same mistakes again.

Ultimately, the more you level up your life - for the benefit of yourself and/or your kids (if you have them) - then the easier dating more *naturally* becomes. Because *so* few men are putting in any sort of effort (at all), the fact that you are **immediately** sets you out from the crowd.

Women are Hypergamous? Of course they are! That's what makes it *even better*. Why do you think the men that are putting the most effort into improving their lives also happen to have access to the most women - by default (or the "top 20%" as the dating apps prove)?

By the way, you can *greatly* diminish (but never *completely* remove) the odds of being #metto'd by simply not being a dick to women. Each time I've let a woman down, they were (nearly) all happy to be friends with me afterwards. I - politely - refused those requests and simply wished the (non batshit crazy) women all the very best in life. The bat-shit crazy ones I blocked immediately.

Look, if you want to opt-out from dating then, as with everything in life, you do you. And I *sincerely* hope you get to live your best life - regardless of how you choose to live it.

However, having personally experienced the company of multiple women who have shown a **genuine** burning desire for me, I'm happy to continue to enjoy a - feminine - woman's company. Sure, I may go without a woman (or sex) for a while in the future. But that's no biggie anymore. I have a true abundance mindset that transcends *every* area of my life now.

9

PROMISCUOUS PRIMATES

Most men idealize a single type of relationship with women. The version that Walt Disney and culture sold us as kids.

One man, his wife, their children, and eternal love.

Society has conditioned us to believe that a relationship is going to be nice, romantic, caring, and respectful. That we'll find that "one good girl" that will only date and love you. That you'll both get engaged, then get married, have kids and live "happily ever after." That she will be a faithful, loving wife and mother "In richer or poorer, in sickness or in health. 'til death do us part."

This is a social contract that very rarely fulfills its promise of a blissful life. Instead, marriage comes with significant risks to men.

While the next chapter talks about marriage in more depth, it is important to note that this social contract is exceedingly difficult to manage over the long term.

Our highly promiscuous ancestors lived as non-monogamous hunter/gatherers, in small nomadic tribes, and preceded us by six million years. We've lived as modern humans for 200,000 years, and civilization, as we know it, began around 6,000 years ago. Monogamy and marriage have only been around for less than 2,000 years.

Men and women are, by nature, highly promiscuous. There's also a massive conflict between how we've all been told to behave, versus our instinctual hard-wiring. Which has been built up over millions of years of evolution.

In this chapter, I want to expose some myths about humans and enlighten you to the true nature of our sexual strategies.

We are terrible at monogamy

In fact, as a species, we are highly promiscuous. When it comes to mammals, monogamy isn't common at all. In fact, as a sexual strategy, monogamy is an outlier amongst mammals.

I always catch heat from traditional conservatives for talking about how badly we fail at monogamy. But, as the saying goes, a bomber only gets flak when it's over the target.

It's universally accepted by those that study the dynamics between men and women, that the male sexual strategy is unlimited access to unlimited women. Whereas the female sexual strategy is open hypergamy.

What that means is men want to scatter their seed far and wide. As men produce millions of sperm every month, those seeds are both ridiculously cheap and readily available.

Women, however, are more complicated. They look for the best genetic investment in their offspring and the best provisioning male, because their eggs are a limited resource.

You should note that the best genetic investment, and best provisioning male, isn't always the same man. It's sometimes one high value alpha with great genetics that provides the seed, and another, more beta, reliable male that provides for the need of raising the offspring.

Hence the popular soundbite distilling the female sexual of open hypergamy as: "Alpha fucks; Beta bucks."

A woman's sexual strategy is dualistic and quite frustrating for most men to comprehend. It's also why men often raise grievances about women crying over wanting "Mr. Dependable," while she goes off and fucks "Mr. Exciting" instead.

How her sexual strategy constantly changes

To further complicate the matter for men, it must be understood that a woman's sexual strategy changes over time. Under the age of 27, women are generally in their party years, and are happy to explore, and sleep with, as many high value alpha men as possible. By the time she is in her late twenties, she has reached the "Epiphany Phase" of her life. This is where millions of years of evolution in her DNA yell at her, "Hey lady, where are the babies!?".

The "Epiphany Phase" is often when women will start seeking out a suitable man to have children with. Ideally, they want a strong alpha seed, and a tender beta protector. But these traits rarely exist in the same man, and high value alphas aren't that easy for her to lock down. So, recognizing the urgency of the matter because both her fertility, and beauty are diminishing assets as she ages, women will often compromise and settle for a more beta male that they deemed as "good enough."

It's why you'll often see many mid-thirties divorced women on the dating market with kids in tow after initiating her divorce. I encountered many of these women on the dating market after my own divorce. I also noticed a trend of some version of the soundbite: "I loved him, but I wasn't IN love with him anymore."

Somehow, today he is a loser at worst, and inadequate at best. But, at some point in time, he was good enough for her.

This completely violates the marriage vows of "To have and to hold from this day forward, for better, for worse, for richer, for poorer, in sickness and in health, to love and to cherish, 'til death do us part..."

What's the point in subscribing to this notion, if 50% of marriages end in divorce, 80% of divorces are initiated by women and of those that remain together less than 13% remain in a state of love?

Where is the love and commitment?

I've coached many men who have taken this hook, line, and sinker. However, you need to understand that marriage is no buffer from hypergamy. If a woman feels like she hasn't done the best that she can do, and her Sexual Market Value (or SMV) has increased over her partner's significantly, then the marriage is at risk. Women can, and often do, leave the perfectly good men that they took those vows with, so they can "Go and explore their options."

This is often around the time when she'll get her breast augmentation, start hitting the gym and yoga studio, and why wouldn't she? She's had kids, so family law ensures she'll be well looked after financially. There's also plenty of people, and western culture telling her: "You go girl, you don't need a man, and you can do better."

Her cycles

When women ovulate, they dress more provocatively, wear more make-up, and expose more skin. It's when they prefer men with signals of higher testosterone, more facial symmetry, a deeper voice, who's taller, who has bigger muscles and, of course, a real alpha presence. Basically, the "alpha fucks" part of the hypergamy equation. But, when women are on their period, their preference for men shifts more towards comfort, provisioning, and safety. Essentially, the "Beta Bucks" part of hypergamy.

The reality is society, religion, government, school, media, culture, and family have programmed us as men to look for "the one" and then only be with her. But, when you observe the behavior of human's sexual strategy, it's more or less "monogomish."

We rarely pair bond to one partner for life. Instead, we try to declare monogamy to one partner at a time, while acting clandestine in our adulterous adventures. Humans usually have multiple sexual partners and relationships throughout our lives.

At some point, you'll learn the hard way that women are not particularly good at being monogamous over the long term. Although, neither are men.

Women can, and do, move very quickly from partner to partner. In several cases, I've known women who've slept with multiple partners, while 'committed,' in a 24-hr period as they felt that it advanced their sexual strategy. All without giving your feelings or ego investments into a relationship with her a second thought.

I'm personally aware of women doing this at least twice in my life.

Sex at Dawn

In Chris Ryan's pivotal 2011 book 'Sex at Dawn', he examines human promiscuity throughout history on a deep level. All evolutionary evidence, and the terrible success record of marriage today, points to both men and women being incredibly poor at long term monogamous pair bonding.

Here are some shocking evolutionary truths about humans and our primate cousins we share 98% of our DNA with:

Male and female size differentials

Only non-monogamous primates universally have males that are 15-20% larger than females. In harem-based primates (like Gorillas), the size differential is even more pronounced, with the male being twice the size of the female. In monogamous based primates, like Gibbons, there's no size differential between males and females.

Penis and testicle size

Only non–monogamous and promiscuous primates have large testicles and a highly specialized penis to facilitate sperm competition in the reproductive tract of the female. Humans, by comparison to most primates by body weight, have large testicles, and very large penises. Harem- based primates, like Gorillas, have tiny testicles the size of kidney beans, and unspecialized penises smaller than your pinky finger. This is because the silverback owns the reproductive rights to his harem of females through sheer physical strength and size.

There is no need for the sperm to "fight it out" in the reproductive tract for the rights to fertilize the egg. The fighting is finished long before any other male can get anywhere near the reproductive tracts of his harem females. Larger testicles are a consequence of sperm competition in the reproductive tracts and is most common in non-monogamous primates.

Female Copulatory Vocalization

Of the hundreds of primate species (including humans), female copulatory vocalization (aka loud moaning during sex) universally exists through non-monogamous primates only. In monogamous based primates, like the Gibbons for example, there is no moaning from the females during sex.

Remember that the next time you are having sex, because millions of years of evolution are making her moan as a calling to other males to mate with her. This reduces the chances of infanticide, since it is impossible for the males to know who the father is. It also ensures that the female obtains the highest quality sperm to compete for her single available egg in her reproductive tract.

Sex that doesn't lead to pregnancy

On average, non-monogamous promiscuous primates have sex 750 times, or more, for every pregnancy. In humans, it's approximately 1,000 times for every pregnancy. Sex for the purpose of pleasure and socializing is very unusual in the animal world. Yet, it's quite common in non-monogamous primates. For most animals they have sex, on average, 10-15 times for every pregnancy that occurs.

Humans rarely have sex just to reproduce. If you factor in all the ways humans have sex that can't possibly lead to pregnancy (for example, oral and anal), then over 99% of the sex humans have will never lead to a pregnancy. Sex for non-monogamous promiscuous primates is all about social interaction, pleasure, validation, connection, or transactions.

Cuckoldry

Cuckoldry, or "cuck", is a term that is often used online to be disparaging. It's where a man raises another man's child (his genetic investment). Note, that 43% of North American children are being raised by a single mother. So, it needs to be stated that most of these children are the result of a woman taking on the alpha seed for the best genetic material.

She then pivots her sexual strategy, either by choice, or involuntarily, to beta need. Therefore, finding a willing male to adopt her offspring, either knowingly or unknowingly.

There are millions of these women on dating sites today looking for beta cucks to take over the responsibility of raising another man's child. In fact, some are even brazen enough to go shopping for their cuckold, while pregnant with another man's seed.

There is another, less obvious, form of cuckoldry today, and it is beta men unknowingly experiencing paternity fraud from raising children he thought were his. However, the kids are in fact the alpha male's seed.

Marriage is no buffer from paternity fraud. It's impossible to determine the actual statistics because fraud, by definition, requires deceit, something women are highly evolved at. However, it's estimated that anywhere from 10-30% of children that are born are not biologically the child of the man that is acting as the "father" to that child.

The female primary social order is so vested in burying paternity fraud by women, that feminist groups have called it "the demonization of women." In fact, paternity testing in some countries has been outlawed by the feminine imperative.

Men's proclivity to "Oneitis"

Of the hundreds of men that I've coached, one of the most common reasons for booking a call was to deal with a condition known as "Oneitis." We loosely define Oneitis as when a guy falls hard for a girl, to the point of an unhealthy obsession over her.

It is often characterized by the guy making a statement such as: "She's the only one for me."

One shortcoming of the male belief system is that there is only one perfect woman for us. Women will argue that they feel oneitis too. But, it's never anywhere near close to the debilitating degree of "Oneitis" that I've seen men suffer from.

It's a scarcity mindset and is something I've personally experienced in the past. I've pined for at least two women that I believed were "the one."

Men suffering from "Oneitis" can't sleep properly or focus on tasks. They lose weight because of a lack of appetite and are distracted from chasing excellence. The sulking they do can last for weeks, months, or in some cases, for well over a year.

I've done it myself and I can honestly say it's one of the most pathetic things I've done and see men do.

There's a lot of theories floating around about why men suffer so badly from it. But, as there are over four billion women on the Earth, it's incredibly arrogant to think there is just one perfect woman for you.

But you can't tell that to the guy who's curled up in a ball crying himself to sleep, because he got dumped by his "Oneitis," and that he needs to let it go and move on. He genuinely cannot fathom a world without her.

So, how does a man reduce his tendency for 'Oneitis'? By creating abundance and options in his life. In short, he spins plates, and makes himself his own mental point of origin.

Enter plate theory

We've all seen the circus act of the man spinning multiple plates on several sticks. If not, it works like this: The circus performer randomly makes some spinning inputs to each plate. He then gives each plate some attention as they need it, enabling them to spin simultaneously, but independently.

A "plate" is any woman you are dating non-monogamously while also seeing other women.

When spinning plates, you are not obligated to be intimate with more than one woman, but if you are so inclined, you may. This dating strategy is especially ideal because:

- It creates plenty of contrast in female nature, and helps men looking for an LTR, or a mother for children, to assess the best possible candidate. Red flags become clear when you have options.
- It creates an abundance mindset and greatly reduces the chances of "Oneitis" from occurring.
- It helps men optimize their sexual strategy of unlimited access to unlimited women.
- You remain your own mental point of origin.
- You can quickly eliminate the women with a lower interest in you, because they won't tolerate being an option to a man that is dating other women.
- It helps quickly solidify women with a strong

interest in you, because they will tolerate other women in your life.

A lot of men think that women won't tolerate being treated as a plate. However, we know by watching what women do, that many women are - genuinely - happier to share a high value alpha than to be saddled with a faithful beta loser.

Men already in a monogamous relationship, or marriage, cannot spin plates. But for men, especially under the age of 30, this is ideal to help them more rapidly understand the sexual marketplace, and what drives arousal and desire between the sexes.

Men post-divorce, recently single, or otherwise, should also consider this dating strategy. Because any immediate commitment to one woman after you've been through the divorce machine usually ends in a train wreck.

I've seen plenty of men not give themselves enough time to understand female nature, only to rush straight into another LTR or marriage without updating their belief system. These men often get into several marriages and then wonder why women keep taking them to the cleaners.

Taking some time to date casually and spin plates will help recalibrate your awareness on the sexual marketplace.

A man should never openly declare that he is spinning plates. Rather he should, through his actions, covertly convey that he is a man of status. That he has options by the choices he makes, and the availability in his schedule.

For example, if you normally see a plate on Wednesday nights, and she wants to add a Friday night (but you have plans with another date), then you simply respond with "I have plans, but I'll see you next Wednesday." You don't need to explain what you are doing, why, or with whom.

In fact, what this will do is induce competition anxiety in her head. Which, if she's hot for you, will increase her desire for you as she'll see you as a man of higher value who has his time in demand by others.

One of the greatest aphrodisiacs for women, especially those with desire for you, is the unknown, and letting her marinate on rationalizing your whereabouts often increases desire in women.

Once again, women would rather share a high value alpha than be saddled with a faithful loser. **You**, an unplugged man who's continuously working hard on leveling-up his life, are the prize - so act like it.

Spin those plates

A man up to his late twenties should ideally never limit his options to just one woman, or get into a LTR. Most men have no idea what women are about, or understand their nature, and are incapable of staying focused on building their purpose in life. Far too many men in their twenties are too quick to abandon their purpose in life. Instead, they want to fulfill that narrative of having a girlfriend, or worse a wife, for definition. Women should never define you.

If you do allow a woman to enter your frame, and be a part of your life, then you should only ever allow it if she compliments your life. She must not be the focus of it.

I've noticed, during coaching, that there are many men that had moved across the country in their twenties, changed their majors, and knocked up their girlfriend. All because they thought it was a good idea. Only to get divorced at thirty-five, get forced through the family law meat grinder, and end up with no access to his kids. It's at this point where they book a coaching call with me to guide them out the other end with the least amount of damage.

So slow things down and stop acting like women are a scarce resource (because they're not).

High value men that are competent, resourceful, and know how to make serious money are a scarce resource. Beautiful women aren't.

The ROI on chasing excellence is far greater than chasing women, more so when you know nothing about female nature.

Spinning plates will lead to some Friends With Benefits (or, FWB). An FWB arrangement is loosely defined as a non-monogamous friendship with sexual intimacy, but with no dates, sleep overs, or introduction to family or friends.

Ideally, you want a FWB arrangement to last over a prolonged period of time, and you can have more than one FWB. However, they rarely last long and if they do, a FWB can come in, and out, of your life like the seasons. Therefore, don't be surprised if an old fling contacts you well into the future.

There are women you will automatically categorize as a FWB when you identify red flags from that chapter of this book. **DO NOT** allow a woman with red flags to be more than a FWB, it is incumbent on you to assess and filter through women that display red flags.

Don't give a FWB priority in your schedule - she is only an option when your time permits.

A monogamous Long-Term Relationship (LTR)

You should only consider a conventional, monogamous relationship with a woman after you have spun enough plates, and the cream has risen to the top. She must also exhibit none of the warning signs I describe in the '21 Red Flags' chapter. Or, if she does, then she is pro-actively working on fixing that area of her life herself.

Women don't like to admit it, but they are natural plate spinners because of their hypergamous nature.

They are always asking themselves, "Is this the best I can do?". If you are dating a woman, then assume that she is seeing other men, until she initiates the "Where do we stand?" talk and wants to open dialogue about a deeper commitment. Women, not men, should start the "talk" about a long-term relationship.

Never, ever, initiate a "Where do we stand?" talk. It's weak and signals scarcity in your life. Let her bring it up. Remember, women are the gatekeepers to sex, while men are the gatekeepers to relationships. Which means that, while a woman gets to decide when you will be intimate with her; *you* get to decide if you want to become more serious with her (and whether or not it's on an exclusive basis).

You should only consider an LTR after about six months of plate spinning. If she demands, or sets an ultimatum for an LTR after only a month of dating, move on and let her go.

Once again, *men are the gatekeepers to relationships, and women are the gatekeepers to sex.* You, as the man, get to decide when a woman gets your exclusive sexual, and non-sexual, attention. **No-one else**.

If you do this and get into a monogamous LTR, you end up abandoning your male sexual strategy of unlimited access to unlimited women. If that's not for you, and you want the option open on your end for variety, then "the talk" is the time to make the statement clear.

Avoid open relationships on both ends, these new-aged open relationships rarely work, women truthfully don't want other men when they see you as their hypergamous best option. Other men become almost invisible to her when she has genuine burning desire, and the *last* thing you want as a man is to poison the well (*especially* with a woman who's fully in your frame).

You should also note that if you choose to abandon your sexual strategy, then she must also then abandon her sexual strategy of open hypergamy.

That means: No male friends, no more seeking attention on social media with provocative pictures and posts, and no overnight girl's trips to places where she can proclaim to her friends "What happens in Vegas stays in Vegas." These are firm boundaries that you **must** be prepared to hold to protect the sanctity of the relationship.

If she calls you "controlling," or "insecure," remind her that she came to you, chose you, and this is a condition of the relationship. I simply cannot care for, love, or protect a woman that is doing things, intentionally or not, that might compromise our commitment to each other.

Some other conditions that should exist for an LTR to work well for you:

- You should be one to two points higher than her on the SMV scale, so she feels that she's optimizing her hypergamy. Remember, a woman can only be content if she feels like her man is of higher value than her.
- Your frame **must** be the dominant frame of the relationship, meaning that she is a complement to your life, not the focus. A woman that's fully in your frame will defer to you in major choices.
- She must understand, through your covert actions and words, that everyone is replaceable - including her.
- There is no "one." You, on the other hand, must understand that you never own her, it's just your turn. She may be in your life for a year, or she may be with you until "death do you part." But *every* relationship ends at some point.
- On a scale of one to 10, with 10 being the highest level of interest, her interest level in you must be an obvious nine (but preferably a 10). Women with an interest level lower than that will be an exceptional amount of work, and the chances of her love wandering will be higher.
- You must have done some recon work on her family and friends and decided if they are people you enjoy being around. This is because she will always, regardless of her feelings for you, choose them over the relationship. So, make sure her family and friends are good people and that you like being around them. Most importantly, if you

are planning on marriage and kids, then look at her mother. She will eventually look like, and behave like, her.

- Also, refrain from living with an LTR, as doing so causes her competition anxiety to relax, making it tougher for you to manage the frame of the relationship. The only exception to this is if you are planning on having children and you need to vet her as a mother by living together first.

A long-term relationship with a woman brings considerably more work to a man's life when it comes to managing the frame of the relationship. However, an excellent woman can add substantial value to your life.

At the time of updating this book, I'm still in the same non-cohabiting LTR. My woman is quite a bit younger than me. She's tidy, non-materialistic, loves to cook healthy meals, is generally positive, very sexual, fun loving, and has a great relationship with her father and my child. If she didn't add any value to my life, I wouldn't have bothered to enter into an LTR with her.

Once again. A woman must **always** be a complement to your life and not the focus. If you want an excellent relationship with a woman (or women), then this should be *every* man's non-negotiable.

If you ignore my advice and allow the red flags (which I cover in this book) into your life, or even live with your LTR, you *will* expose yourself (and your wealth) to the risks of family law, and those red flags will make your relationship miserable.

In most Western countries, the state deems you to be in a common law marriage after one to two years. And, even if you aren't legally married, she may *still* have rights to half of your assets. Therefore, it's **essential** that you consult with a family lawyer in your state or province before you live with any woman. If you have more assets than her, then see if you can protect them with a cohabitation agreement.

The tattoo test

If you really want to test my theories on the "soulmate myth" that men subscribe to, and how willing she is to enter your frame in an LTR, then the tattoo test is brilliant. It really forces her to show, via her actions, that she is serious about an LTR with you over the long haul.

If she starts "the talk", it usually encompasses some version of the soundbites: "I'll love you forever, and ever" or, "We were made for one another."

Lovingly tell her, "Good, prove it. Tattoo my name on your body."

It doesn't need to be visible, or huge. Most of the time, she will make the tattoo discrete, so it's hidden in her bikini or bra line. Don't force it on her or march her into a tattoo studio. Instead, just drop the hint, but be serious about it, and then see what she does.

This is not a two-way street either. You are not tattooing her name on you. She is the one that is asking for your exclusive attention, love and resources. A woman who's in your frame that sees you as a high value alpha, and that has a genuine, burning desire for you shouldn't protest and would love to have your name on her body.

A woman that doesn't see you as her best option, and her "forever" man, will make up excuses.

Regardless of what they are, whatever excuses she makes, she is telling you she doesn't really believe that you are her best option. You're not satisfying her hypergamous needs, and she doesn't see you two together forever.

Remember, whenever there is a conflict between her actions, and words, always, always believe what she does. As the old saying goes: "Actions speak louder than words".

Open LTR

The LTR can either be open, or closed. So, you can either be exclusive with your LTR, or keep the relationship open where you continue to have one or two other women that you see periodically. But she should understand that you are doing this.

Covertly spinning plates while in an LTR always catches up to you somewhere down the line. You'll end up dealing with a lot of unnecessary drama in your life.

There is nothing wrong with an open LTR, aside from societal conditioning telling you to be monogamous.

She can also be in an open LTR with you, but now you are leaning into Polyamory (Poly), and a more beta frame of a relationship.

The highest value alpha males will be in an open LTR on their end, but she can't do the same. More feminized men will gawk at this statement and protest. But, throughout history, truly high value alpha men had a harem of women that were sexually exclusive with him.

Polyamory

The "Poly Lifestyle" is being pushed by the media, and even some academics seem to like to push the narrative since they are in a poly marriage. If you are unfamiliar with the "Poly Lifestyle", you let your wife or girlfriend have sex with whoever they want, while you also do what you want. It's basically an open LTR for both of you.

This dating strategy is becoming the standard for many beta males because they would rather share a woman versus not having one at all.

On the surface, it may look appealing. However, men and women aren't equal. More often than not, it's two beta males fighting over one girl. All while she goes out on the weekends sleeping with the alphas for fun (leaving the poly men to raise her kid(s)).

Successful and influential men throughout history have generally run a harem of women. Ishmail 'the bloodthirsty,' a Moroccan Sultan from the 1600s, had nine wives, hundreds of concubines, and the total number of children is unknown, but speculated to be at least 1,000. He also hired men he made Eunuchs to guard his harem females.

Genghis Khan was another historical figure that spread his seed far and wide, with .5% of the male population today carrying his Y chromosome.

This story of successful, strong, influential, and rich men is common throughout our history, yet I can't find any records of women running a harem. Food for thought.

In Conclusion

We live in a strange time where western society generally tends to enforce monogamy and frowns upon promiscuity. Yet, human behavior is exceptionally promiscuous, and when we get to picking the mother for our kids, it is rarely with a virgin. Most women today have slept with dozens of men prior to settling down.

Evolutionarily speaking, it would seem that we are adapted for both monogamish and polygyny mating. When you look at how we have evolved and operate today, there is a lot of flip flopping back and forth.

Large testicles would indicate a multi-mate strategy (like chimps & bonobos) and probably how we lived for millions of years as nomadic hunter gatherers. However, our testicles are slightly smaller than our primate cousins today, by a percentage of body mass and, since the advent of agriculture 10,000 years ago, they seem to be getting smaller as we have evolved away from that lifestyle..

But we still have much larger testicles than Gorillas, so we aren't exactly a haram-based species. Then when you look at female copulation during sex, the obvious size differences between human males and females, and how women will cuckold men into raising another man's seed and things get awfully complicated when these facts point towards non monogamy.

True monogamy doesn't seem to exist in human mating, as it does in the animal kingdom because, otherwise, we would stay with our first intimate mate forever.

When it comes to the types of relationships you can have with women, I *strongly* encourage you to always make yourself your own mental point of origin. This means you do what is right - for YOU. Men should always set the frame of the relationship at the beginning, because it's the exit that women most often control.

If monogamy is your path, then make sure you chose it, and it hasn't been forced on you by your woman or society. Natural monogamy can work, but only if it is organic, and you both truly want to be sexually exclusive. I would strongly encourage all men to use the tattoo test if you are going to start an LTR. This test will assure you that her actions truly do align with her words.

Chris Ryan once said:

 "Monogamy is like going vegan. You can choose a plant-based diet, but that doesn't mean bacon will stop smelling good."

The cold hard truth

Never forget:

- Women may be the gatekeeper of who they have sex with, but you are the gatekeeper of who you have a relationship with. And, as a man of increasingly high value, that's the strongest, and most valuable, bargaining chip of the two.
- When a woman has a genuine desire for you, and appreciates your value, then she will have no

problems sharing you with other women as you are satisfying her hypergamous nature.

- Track the menstrual cycle of any potential LTRs.
- Watch how differently they behave when they are ovulating, versus when they are menstruating.
- I've said it before, and I'll say it again, always believe a woman's actions over her words. Her actions will tell you what her true priority is, while telling you the truth about how she *truly* feels.
- As noted by my good friend Dr. Shaun T. Smith in his book "The Tactical Guide to Women," spend as much time as possible vetting and setting healthy boundaries with a woman before committing. It's from month 18-onwards when a woman's *true* personality comes through.

Steve From Accounting's Field Report

It's definitely been harder for me to find women who don't, more than likely, have a body count that's into the double figures these days. However, I've also found a way (that works for me) to unapologetically tell a woman that I won't be exclusive to her.

I do this pretty much from the outset, as my time is limited in availability and I also see no value in telling a woman what she wants to hear just to get her into bed. It also allows me to define the frame of how I'm living my life and she gets the subtext pretty quickly that I don't fuck around and have no fear of being honest and straight with her (which, believe it or not, actually **builds** more trust in her).

If a woman has a **true** genuine burning desire for you (and NPD/BPD women can *certainly* fake that for a short while), then there's a **very** high probability that she'll accept that she's not going to be the only one you'll be sleeping with (I always emphasize the fact that I will remain "discreet, and very safe," which has certainly helped cut-off many potential fears that they may have).

The RP adage "She'd rather share a high value man than be saddled with a faithful loser" is actually very accurate (which surprised the hell out of me the first few times I got women to understand the fact that I wouldn't be exclusive with them).

However, doing so requires having absolutely **zero** fear that she'd say no and leave (which is always a distinct possibility - and a few women I briefly dated wouldn't accept that - which was fine). If you have a scarcity mindset *at all*, then this won't work. You *genuinely* have to be ready to let them walk away (while wishing them well in their lives).

You'll tend to find that, as long as you're doing the work and are *clearly* leveling up past the other men in the local dating market, then it's *far* easier for you to be upfront about how you are living your awesome life - without needing to be a dick about it.

10

WHY GENUINE BURNING DESIRE MATTERS

One of the simplest concepts a man must understand is "genuine desire." What it is, why it matters, and how to measure it. When you get it right, it's a superpower. But, when you get it wrong, it leads you to making terrible choices, leading to poor results with women.

A man will chase a woman who's indifferent to him and suddenly wife her up. Only to find out, after two kids and seven years of investing his blood, sweat, and tears into the relationship, she's leaving him for another man. A man she has more desire for, while simultaneously running him hard through the divorce machine.

In 2018 I recorded a video in my car while heading home from the office, talking about why genuine burning desire matters with women. To find this video, search 'genuine burning desire' on my channel.

I've created a simple system to make it easier to determine her interest in you.

How to determine her interest

I've been using a measurement system in my business for over 10-years now called the "Net Promoter Score" (or NPS). It's a system which uses a measurement scale of 1 - 10. The system highlights three distinct levels of interest that a potential customer has in your business.

You survey your customers with the question: "On a scale of 1 - 10, how likely are you to recommend our services to a friend or colleague?" When you plug in a formula after conducting your customers' surveys, it tells you how much interest your customers have in your business.

The levels of interest are:

- A score of 9 to 10: These customers are your "Promoters" and they love what you do.
- A score of 7 to 8: These customers are indifferent. They have nothing good, nor bad, to say about you.
- And finally, a score of 1 to 6: These customers are your "Detractors" and they don't like you.

You may wonder why I am applying a business measurement tool to a man's life.

It's because the answers to most of the struggles we have already existed elsewhere. We simply need to identify them and then apply what works.

However, we aren't interested in the NPS of you as a man. That would require sampling every woman you've either dated, or are currently dating, to find out what your NPS would be. It's impractical to survey so many women with such a question and expect an honest reply. But understanding how to measure desire is important and you must know why genuine burning desire matters.

Let me break down the way desire works for you:

A Score of 9 - 10 shows Genuine Burning Desire

When a woman truly desires you, you'll know it. She'll show up on time and call or text you without you making the first attempt. She'll also respond quickly, willingly enter your frame, and complement your life (without wanting to be the focus of it).

She will also ask you questions to get to know you better. She may also buy you random gifts, make you meals, and follow you closely on social media. She will even message you first on a dating app, always responding quickly. She will show up for dates with make-up and nice clothes, she'll enthusiastically fuck your brains out and swallow your load.

She will also often initiate sex with you, unprovoked. When a woman genuinely desires you, it will be as obvious as taking a blow from a frying pan to the forehead.

A Score of 7 - 8 shows Indifference

When women are indifferent, they frequently reschedule/cancel dates, ask for more than they give, become bitchy, and sometimes confrontational. She will shit test you often, take longer to respond to your texts/calls, not put much effort into her appearance when you see her, and she will rarely ask you questions to get to know you.

If you message her on a dating app, she'll be slow to respond. Her interest in the bedroom will also not be very high either. She'll be far less likely to want to suck your cock and she'll rarely initiate sex with you. When a woman is indifferent to you, it will be obvious.

A Score of 1 to 6 shows they're a Detractor

When women are detractors, they will not respond to your calls or texts, and they will not go out on dates with you. They will not follow you on social media, and if you message them on dating apps, they will not respond. When a woman is a detractor, it will be obvious.

Every man, when dealing with a woman on a romantic level, should always gauge her interest in him by watching her behavior. He must respond accordingly by only allocating his valuable time, energy, and resources on the woman who shows him a strong, genuine, burning desire.

Be attractive, not unattractive

Men are natural problem solvers. So, your next logical question is: "How do I create such an enthusiastic desire in her, so she signals a clear indicator of interest in me?".

The answer is that you can't manufacture it. It must be natural. You must be a man that is desirable. You must be a man that exudes confidence, competence, and strength.

It's unlikely that a woman with only a detractor level of interest in you will ever enthusiastically become a promoter and want to fuck you.

It's not that it can't happen. I've had plenty of women over the years, from my past, that may have been passively interested in me back then, only to express a much higher desire later on down the road as my "Sexual Market Value" (or SMV) had greatly improved. This often happens when she deems that her SMV has gone down as "The Wall" does its work. All while watching your SMV go up as you approach your own SMV peak later in life.

For a definition of what "The Wall" is, check out the Glossary at the back of the book.

However, at the end of the day, you must ask yourself why would you want to get involved with a woman that gave her best to someone else, making you her second choice.

The genuine burning desire you receive from a woman must be organic. You cannot manufacture it or negotiate it. Anytime you negotiate desire, you get obligated compliance in return, which only leads to resentment further down the line.

You can, however, work on yourself. In fact, it is the only part of the universe that you can control. If you are fat, fix it. If you are broke, fix it. If you don't understand "game", learn it. If you are socially insignificant, learn to become influential.

These aspects are truly within your control. Some men will argue that they are short and that their height is out of their control. True, but if you aren't tall, then do the work to be a fit, rich, smooth, short badass.

If you are not a high value man that commands a high level of attention, then you cannot expect a "10" to want to rip off your clothes enthusiastically and jump your bones.

Your highest "Return on Investment" (or ROI) in life will always be that of being a man of vision, purpose, and who is always chasing excellence.

Gauging your SMV

Ask yourself the question: "On a scale of 1 to 10, with 10 being the absolute best version of myself, and with 1 being the worst, where would I place myself right now?"

It's important to note that you aren't comparing yourself to anyone else - it's only about you.

A perfect 10 would mean that you have already achieved the level of wealth, self-care, success, income, desirability, social recognition, and community that you couldn't do much better. You live where you want, drive cars you love, take vacations when and where you want. You look masculine and strong, women are constantly seeking your attention, and you never worry about money.

If you are rating yourself a six or lower, then I'd suggest limiting your dating, or perhaps stop dating entirely, and go fix yourself before you go chasing after women.

Your ROI on the time invested with women will be low and you will probably become frustrated with your results.

Because of hypergamy, women always seek men who are a few points higher than them on the SMV scale. So, as a man, you have the burden of performance to do the work on yourself.

Remember: "Men are made; women are born." You need to do the work on yourself if you want to be successful with women. Never forget that women have always viewed men as success objects, whereas men have always viewed women as sex objects.

Validational sex versus transactional sex

Women with a high level of desire for you will have sex with you for validation. They crave it, and it's enthusiastic. When women have validational sex, the risk of her claiming either a #MeToo or a false rape claim allegation, after the fact, is almost zero.

I've seen women who crave that validational sex from me drive 45-minutes, in the middle of the night, during a work week, and throw down a dark towel to fuck me enthusiastically on their period.

When women fuck a man for validation, her vagina is soaking wet, your bed will be wet, she will do anything to please you, including swallowing your load, or do anal first, and then swallow your load. There is virtually no limit to what a woman will do with a man that she has an enthusiastic and genuine desire for.

Indifferent women will either have transactional sex with you, or try to use it as a negotiation tool. It's women that have transactional sex that are more likely to claim a #MeToo, or false rape accusation against you. Just because they regretted their choice at a later date.

When women have transactional sex with you, her vagina isn't soaking wet. She won't do much in bed and it will often come with some requirements in exchange for the intimacy she's "giving you." There's a growing trend amongst beta men who are resigned to doing "choreplay".

The Unplugged Alpha (2nd Edition)

"Choreplay" is defined as a man who is doing the household chores that the female would normally do, in exchange for sex.

Simply put, you cannot negotiate genuine desire with a woman. Once you start down the path of transactional sex, the clock starts counting down to the end of the relationship.

If a woman won't do something sexual then, in your head, add "with you" to the end of her statement when she declines it. For example, when she says: "I won't do anal." then add "with you" to the end. Make no mistake about it, she will enthusiastically do it for validation with a man that she has a genuine, burning desire for.

In Conclusion

It's absolutely vital that you only invest your limited time in women whose actions show you, beyond any doubt, that she has nothing but a genuine, burning desire for you. However, never forget that the "Burden of Performance" always rests firmly at your feet. It's up to you, and no-one else, to become the top-tier man that commands that level of genuine desire from a high value woman.

The cold hard truth

Never forget:

- Your highest ROI in life will always be that of being a man of vision, purpose, and who is always chasing excellence.
- Negotiated desire only ever leads to resentment, from both parties, down the road.
- Rest assured, once you've experienced the pleasures of a woman who displays a genuine desire and attraction to you, it'll be easy for you to spot anything less from that point on.

Steve From Accounting's Field Report

The difference between an obligation-led relationship and one where the woman has that genuine, burning desire for you is *unbelievably* clear. You **really** can't go back to a mediocre relationship anymore once you finally find a woman whose boxes you - naturally - check off like they're going out of fashion.

For example, the woman that I've been casually seeing the longest continues to drive to me (45-minutes each way) twice a week to see me at my home. I've **never** been to her house. If I can't see her (due to other commitments), I don't get an ounce of shit or any passive aggressive nonsense from her.

She often buys new lingerie for me to take her out of, she'll gladly pick up anything I ask for from the shops on her way to mine. She'll let me do *anything* to her in the bedroom *without me needing to ask her*. She gladly washes up the dishes for me after I've cooked and will make my bed without asking in the morning.

And the sex has *only gotten better* as time goes on. Seriously. (Massive shout outs to both the Sex God Method 2.0 book and to Stirling Cooper's YouTube videos and online courses - they're all *exceptionally* effective).

Also, I've told her that I will sleep with other women as well (discreetly and very safely) and she's not only accepted it, but she's *also* told her parents *and* her close friends about it! *And she's never been happier!*

Having said that, I *do* enjoy rewarding her by sometimes inviting her to join me on a few trips I had planned to go on. She's now experienced many, *many* "firsts" with me and she's never shown anything but genuine gratitude for that.

It's honestly like I've stepped into a different dimension when I compare it to how my marriage was (which isn't surprising considering I was an unattractive man-child for the vast majority of it). Sadly, there's a few too many areas of her life that I don't wish to invite into mine (keeping her out of LTR territory), but as she's more than happy for things to remain as they are, then we can both enjoy it for as long as it lasts (which we both know won't be forever).

However, it **is** critical to be able to discern the difference between the genuine desire coming from a healthy woman, from that of an unhealthy woman (think cluster-B personality types). Mentally unhealthy women will try and fake the desire to suck you in initially. I had a woman who was very local to me try that shit. Unfortunately for her, my ex-wife educated me on all the tell-tale signs and I **immediately** bailed out of there once she made it clear she wasn't legit.

I've also learned that a relationship doesn't have to be "hard work." It absolutely *can* be effortless. However, that *does* require you to unapologetically be on your purpose, working hard at smashing life, and ultimately maintaining a **rock-solid** frame throughout.

Think about it. Your time with a woman only becomes "hard work" when she's trying to get out of your frame (or when you're constantly failing her to-be-expected shit/compliance tests). If she's *willingly* remaining within **your** frame, then why would it be "hard work"? It isn't. It remains effortless *because* you're retaining your frame throughout.

However, don't expect to naturally tick the hypergamous boxes of women if you're not getting your life in order. That's you being as deluded as the 3rd Wave Feminists who think they can lockdown a "high value" man while bringing nothing of true long-term value to the table.

These days, if I sense a woman isn't showing true desire for me when I'm chatting to her online via a dating app, or when we're chatting face-to-face, then I'll simply wish her well and leave it be right there.

Look, your time is the most valuable resource in your life. **Stop** wasting it on women that don't see you as their best option and keep on leveling-up every area of your life in the meantime. Then, when you *do* find such a woman (and they're definitely out there), watch how she positively reacts to your naturally dominant frame. You won't believe the differences either.

WOMEN'S RULES - WHO THEY MAKE THEM AND BREAK THEM FOR

There is plenty of debate on what constitutes an alpha male and how to become more like one. Most men have heavy ego investments in what they believe and dictate what is what. So, I think it's pointless to get into those.

Instead, I'd like to defer to women. Which, as we already know, are the sexual selectors and, unlike the advice they give to men about women, their behavior won't ever lie to us.

In my life, I've been both the alpha and the beta. And it depended on how effectively my belief system was operating, and also the lens in which I was viewing the world. From my personal experience, and the many men I've coached, women will always break the rules for a man she believes to be alpha.

Like the cute "good girl" librarian that made you patiently wait three months for basic missionary sex when you were 20. She'll end up naked in bed with Chad Thundercock 15-minutes after meeting him in Ibiza at the foam cannon party on her 23rd birthday. You can also be certain she'll be doing everything she said she wouldn't do with you - with him.

Never forget: Women break rules for alphas and make them for betas.

If every alpha had a dime for every time a woman said, "I don't normally do this," when it comes to first date sex, sex without a condom, swallowing, or some other act she might later regret, these men would be rich.

When women say: "I don't do that," always add to it in your head: "With you." Because she'll enthusiastically do it with a man who she deems worthy of such sexual gymnastics.

Women will always break the rules for an alpha. It always has been, and always will be, that way. Conversely, women will MAKE rules for men who they deem to be a mere beta.

They will make a beta wait eight, likely expensive, dates to sleep with them. They won't give a beta man oral, and they certainly won't drive to a bar to meet (because it's too far for her to bother for a beta male). Women *always* make rules for betas.

Enter the Amazonian

It's story time. I once had a first date with a thirty-something woman that I met online. She showed up around 30 lbs heavier than her pictures suggested, and also quite a bit taller than I expected. But she was cute enough to have one drink with, and as I was already there, I proceeded with the date.

Women will subconsciously shit test men all the time to see if they are alpha or beta. So, a few swigs into my beer, and she proceeded to tell me how, after some bad experiences with men, she now has an "eight dates" rule before she'll sleep with them.

Nearly spitting out my beer, I chuckled with amused mastery, and called bullshit. I stated I don't play games and I certainly don't negotiate desire, or when sex happens.

I also told her it was childish, and interferes with the natural progression of the sexual dynamics and genuine desire.

Men need to understand. Anytime you negotiate desire, it *automatically* creates obligated compliance. Which leads to resentment (and nobody wants that).

After some back-and-forth banter on the topic of her "eight

date rule," with a dilation of her pupils, and a huff of her giant tits in her push-up bra, she put down her girly cocktail, and leaned forward to show off her cleavage. She looked me dead in the eyes, smirked, and said "Okay, let's fuck right now." And made a gesture towards the bathrooms in the bar.

The same woman who was previously lecturing me about her "Eight date rule," was ready to bang me in the bathroom. Literally only 20-minutes after I sat down with her.

It's what is called a shit test - and I passed it with flying colors. It was also one of the few times in my life where I've passed on an aggressive sexual female advance.

If a woman is placing hoops for you to jump through, and tests to pass, then she is usually testing you to see where you fit on her Alpha to Beta scale. And, I promise you, it'll not end in amazing "Fuck me like you own me!" sex if you comply with her frame.

A woman will break all her rules if she views you as an alpha. Every. Single. Time.

She will *willingly* enter your frame. She will come to see you. She will gladly swallow your load. She will even have sex with you on her period. She will enthusiastically say "I want to feel you everywhere," and put your cock in her ass. She will make you breakfast in the morning, make your bed, do the laundry. And, ultimately, if you can maintain the frame of such a dynamic on a long-term basis, she will become a compliment to your life.

However, a woman who's making rules for you views you as a beta. Every. Single. Time.

She'll make you wait for sex. You'll go to her. She won't perform oral. You'll be buying her dinner, be her shoulder to cry on, and she'll be the focus of your life. She will treat you like an emotional tampon. She'll use you to fix her car, hang shelves, and take care of her kids. All while she goes out salsa dancing with her girlfriends where she might meet Chad Thundercock one night and then fuck him in the nightclub's bathroom.

Men that operate in a beta frame end up getting cheated on far more than alpha males. They never get her best (in, or out of, the bedroom) and they end up marrying women that will only ever treat them like a plow horse.

As a man that she deems a Beta, you will have little say in family matters, raising the kids, or financial control. You'll go to your job every week while she drops off the kids in her SUV to school or daycare. Before she sits down in a coffee shop, after yoga class, cackling with her friends about how useless their husbands are. They then complain they had to "give" sex to their Beta husband earlier that week, while they pine for their hot yoga instructor.

That same woman could have been in Ibiza for her birthday, enthusiastically fucking two cute Italian guys like a porn star in a gangbang, just moments after she met them at 2am.

The Alpha to Beta conversion process:

> "A woman spends years 'changing' her man, then wonders what happened to the guy she fell in love with."
> - Anon.

This process takes years, and can turn an alpha into a weak beta male - it's often considered to be the process of "Betatization by a thousand concessions". It is one of the many catalysts that leads to the trauma that men suffer, sending them online to seek answers and the truth.

This is a process I've spoken about many times in my videos, and it turns men from a pet she loves and admires, to a plow horse that she sees as nothing more than a utility. A utility that she emotionally abuses and doesn't want to fuck enthusiastically anymore.

If you aren't aware, and you don't control the frame of the relationship, then the chances are, this will happen to you. It will make you weak, soft, poor, and undesirable to your woman.

The process of "Betatization by a thousand concessions" is a genuine threat to you as a man, especially if you cohabitate, or enter into a marriage, or have children.

Because of women's innate hypergamous nature, women aim to marry up to a better man, so he generally earns the bulk of the income in the household. Meaning that the Betatization process could end up costing you a significant part of your past, and even future, wealth in a divorce.

But that's not even the worst part. Since women still get primary custody of children around 80% of the time, most men not only lose their wealth, but also their decision-making capacity around their children. Meaning that they also lose their ability to father them properly.

Becoming a weak beta is one of the most dangerous things that happens to men in LTRs and marriages.

It is a process that women unknowingly facilitate. And men allow it to happen because we, as men, have been told our entire lives to put her on a pedestal and to be less - so that she can become more.

A thousand concessions

The timeline looks something like this: She locks down a man that she admired, wanted to fuck, and be with. Over time, he turns into the beaten down beta plow horse that succumbs to her beck and call. He performs chores hoping for sex, and is who she ultimately no longer wants to fuck - or even desires.

This phenomenon usually starts with: "Honey, put your dark socks in the dark hamper, and your white socks in the white hamper for whites". It then progresses to "Let's go vegan together!" and ends at "I love you, but I'm not in love with you, I want a divorce, so I'm taking the kids to my mother's".

For a perfect illustration of what these Betatized married plow horses look like, pay attention to your next few trips to the grocery store. Now stroll by the baby diaper isle and look for the family doing their shopping.

You will start to see husbands with an exhausted and beaten down look on their faces. Their kids, aged one, three, and five, plus one bun in the oven, are out of control. His, now rotund, wife with her permanent "resting bitch face" scowls at him about how incompetent he is for putting the wrong diapers in the shopping cart.

Once you see this happen, it can't ever be unseen. You will notice these types of men more often around you. At the mall, at your kid's soccer game, and around social gatherings with friends and family.

This husband is the same man that she, many years prior, would look up to and potentially even had enthusiastically rough, monkey sex with. She would proudly present her new "pet" boyfriend for the first time over the holidays before proudly saying to her family, "This is Kevin, the VP of sales I told you all about from work."

Heck, he was probably the same guy she would get in a quarrel with. He would hang up the phone to control the frame because he was subconsciously alpha enough to know when a soft next worked. She likely drove over at 3am that same night, after he hung up on her, to let him fuck her in the ass, something she rarely did, just to calm him down and get back into his good books.

Kevin the VP of sales started out as an alpha but, through a thousand concessions to placate her whims during the length of the relationship, Kevin becomes the Beta.

An alpha does as he pleases, he possesses the traits of: strength, courage, mastery, and honor. Men want to be him; women want to be with him. When women are with him, they will enthusiastically show it.

A beta on the other hand, is on the other end of the spectrum. He is not her first choice; he is an accessory to her life, a utility, a handyman and, in many cases, she'll also treat him like an ATM.

The worst form of beta is the cuckold. Which is the man that gets involved with a single mother, and then willingly raises the children of another man. Or worse, his wife gets knocked up by another man, and he, unknowingly, raises that child as his own.

Women don't divorce alpha men they admire and look up to. They generally leave beta men that become a plow horse to them. As a man, if you want to take on the risk of marriage and kids, then you need to be on your mission, always maintain the frame, and your alpha status.

Remember, in every relationship, one partner enters the other's frame. It is therefore incumbent on you, as the man, to ensure that your woman is in *your* frame. You *cannot* let the balance of that frame shift to her.

Far too many men, get married and actually believe the vows they take: "In sickness, and in health... for richer or for poorer... 'til death do us part."

The fact of the matter is, women divorce men all the time if the circumstances of the marriage change and she now deems you of lesser value to her. If you get fat, go broke, can't hold down a job, or are utterly useless around a house, then a woman reserves her right to untie the marriage knot.

It's why I tell men all the time that taking on a marriage, or LTR, is far more work than simply dating, or spinning plates (and they both come with far more risks).

Never forget that, if you are going to get married or have kids, then it is imperative to control the frame, and do not allow yourself to become a beta male.

The cold hard truth

Never forget:

- Women break rules for alphas and make them for betas.
- As unfair as it may be, the "Burden of Performance" is always on you. This means that you must always be on your A-game when it comes

to frame, game, and leading the relationship (more so if you're married, or in an LTR).

- If you notice her making rules, or setting conditions, on areas such as when she'll have sex with you (for example: "If you ever want to have sex again, then..."), you now know that she definitely sees you as a Beta and that the frame has shifted.

- Learn to say "No." It's a complete sentence that doesn't need any further explanation. If you've been pussy-whipped for years, then she'll likely be surprised. But also intrigued. Expect her to ramp up the shit tests to see if this new, more assertive you, is the real deal. So, you had best make sure it is.

Steve From Accounting's Field Report

I remember being intrigued (and more than a little skeptical) when I was editing this chapter back in 2020. A lot of it seemed to be "wishful thinking." However, having come to - repeatedly - experience much of what Rich talks about here, it's actually scarily accurate.

I gave up *so* many of my own dreams for my ex-wife, that I made many thousands of small concessions throughout our time together. Back then, I had no spine, no boundaries, and *definitely* no balls.

If you happen to spend some of your valuable time with a woman for whom you - naturally - tick off all her hypergamous "boxes" (and then some), then you'll begin to notice that she'll do the vast majority (if not all) of the above. Seriously.

I now look forward to these shit/competency tests, as they offer me an opportunity to either be extra playful with them, or I reaffirm how I'm going to live my life, and I then gently offer them the choice of either stepping into that, or I'll wish them well and we'll go our separate ways.

Now, it's worth being tactful with some aspects. I remember recently going on a date with a woman from my local Salsa class. We were making out in my car outside my house (I told her to come to mine and park there, so I could drive us to our bouldering date), and I discovered that she had *verrrry* sensitive ears - much to her own surprise (and to my delight).

What followed was a **rapid** escalation that resulted in her not only "breaking her own rules," but she took her own rule book of "taking it slow," immediately tore it up, and then set the damn thing on fire.

Turns out, she couldn't believe she did everything that we did on our second date. I could (because I understood she felt a strong attraction to me), but I gently let her go as I could tell she was *really* struggling with it all, ultimately with her wanting me to step into *her* frame - by taking it "super slow." Nope, not for me thanks.

Other women have tried to pull the exclusivity card for sex early on (I told one "That's not what I'm looking for, but if that's what you need, feel free to leave." She looked shocked, then was visibly turned on when she realized I was dead serious, and we slept together that night - without any more challenges - for a few months at least).

However, not every woman will want to fall into your frame. And that's OK. In fact, I let a woman go yesterday and wished her well when she changed her mind about being OK with me not being sexually exclusive with her. She was 31 and just couldn't handle the jealousy that thinking about me sleeping with other women (as well as her) brought up in her. Cool. We'd had our fun, but it wasn't to be. Not a problem.

And this is where Rich's comment about "the cream rises to the top" fits in. You'll quickly see the differences between the women who *will* willingly step into (and want to stay within) your frame, and those that don't.

Also, it doesn't usually matter how "High Value" you are. Not **every** woman you meet will be a good fit for you. And that's OK. Also, don't expect to get it right *all* the time. I still catch myself making stupid decisions that - upon reflection - weren't attractive. No worries, I'm happy to take the L and learn from it for next time.

However, by sub-communicating (in a non-dickish way) that *you* set the standards and the rules for the relationship *you* want (and that you're not afraid to walk away if you don't get it), you'll start to find that a lot more women will respond positively.

Sure, you'll get some more shit tests (designed to test *just* how strong your frame is), but expect them, welcome them, then bat them away with a playful response, and give zero fucks if she likes that or not.

You'll find yourself as surprised as I am at just *how powerful* unapologetically owning how you want to live your life is with women.

12

21 RED FLAGS

On my YouTube channel, I often reference the phrase "She has more red flags than a Chinese communist parade." In this chapter, I want to dive a little deeper into the riskiest red flags that men need to be aware of as they navigate their life around women.

I've made plenty of these mistakes myself and have counseled hundreds of men who've done the same. Therefore, it's *essential*, for your own wellbeing, that you do not ignore these red flags.

Keep in mind that you *can* pursue a deep relationship with a woman who displays any of these red flags. However, in my estimation, the juice simply isn't worth the squeeze, and the risks *far* outweigh any reward.

If you are a woman reading this chapter, and you identify with a red flag, then don't get upset. Instead, like I keep reminding men: work on yourself, take ownership, and seek counseling.

As many men have observed, the wrong woman can ruin your life if you let her in it. Therefore, learning how to spot red flags early is an *essential* skill for men to master. Even though this chapter covers the twenty major ones I've identified, plenty of others exist - so keep your eyes open.

If you choose to involve yourself with any of these types of women, then my advice, unless otherwise stated, is to limit your interaction to a "Friends With Benefits" (or, FWB) relationship and to keep spinning plates. As soon as you identify one or more of these red flags, limit her to plate status, or pass on them and make no further emotional investment in either her, or in a relationship with her.

There are women out there that *will* add value to your life - if you keep the wrong ones out.

I'm also approaching this chapter with the assumption that you are a man of purpose that values his own masculinity, strength, and traditional male competency skills.

Beta men constantly make concessions and excuses, while accepting red flags. Whereas a high value alpha male keeps chasing excellence and his purpose in life. He doesn't let problem women interfere with his life's mission.

Red flag #1 - Daddy issues

If she doesn't have a friendly relationship with her father, or had an acrimonious relationship with him growing up, then she likely has a variety of daddy issues. Whether her mother pushed her dad out of her life, he set boundaries she rebelled against, or that he was absent, or perhaps he was disinterested in being a dad and instead, acted as a piece of furniture in the house.

Either way, any woman that didn't have a solid relationship with a strong, masculine, and virtuous father in her life will not value a masculine, virtuous, alpha unplugged man.

If she didn't value her father, what makes you think she will value you? I've counseled far too many men that have tried far too hard to rescue women with daddy issues. It's *never* worth your time.

Another area of concern with daddy issues is that it's often tied into Borderline Personality Disorder (or, BPD). Women with BPD frequently originate from fatherless homes, which breeds their fear of abandonment. This fear continues as they become adults, where they will presume that they will, once again, be abandoned. They then act out in such a way that will make abandonment certain.

BPD women are so dangerous because they operate in extremes, they can be freaks in the sheets and then immediately act like a classy lady on the street.

A BPD woman can quickly go from hot to frigid cold. Such BPD women can hook a guy in by pretending to be a caring, loving, and nurturing woman. A BPD woman can create the false sense of perfection that makes you say "Wow, a woman who *finally* loves, respects, *and* appreciates me!".

Asking her "Tell me about your parents growing up" early on helps you to identify, and then filter out, women with daddy issues. Remember that you have two ears and one mouth. So, use them in that ratio - ask, *then* listen. She will often tell you her story.

I've had my fair share of experiences with women who had daddy issues and they are *never* worth your time, effort, or resources.

A woman's father is her primary role model growing up and provides the foundation that governs her belief system. And includes the lens in which she views both men and women, and how they should interact.

However, the origin of her issues is irrelevant because, if she expresses disdain for her father, she is unlikely to value men.

Single-mother households, especially feminist ones, are a petri dish for today's women with daddy issues. A feminist-identifying mother will instill toxic values in her daughter. Instead of valuing you, you'll be deemed as a "privileged male" and will be resented for your masculinity.

After my divorce, I dated a woman who had three older siblings. Her mother became a widow before my ex-girlfriend was born. Instead of being a single mother of three, she optimized her hypergamy and looked for a beta provider. She eventually had a fourth child, my ex-girlfriend, with her second husband.

My ex's mother died of cancer while she was in her early twenties. When I asked about her relationship with her father, she claimed unforgivable indiscretions that her father was responsible for. She painted her mother as a feminist saint and her father as an abusive, misogynist cheater, and child abuser.

While we were dating, my ex went almost twenty years without contact with her father. She unsurprisingly identified as a feminist, became a single mother of two herself, and subsequently had little regard for men and masculinity - unless it served value to her and her children. She then dismissed them once she capitalized on their value.

While she constantly battled her internal conflict to find a high value man, she also resented masculine energy and claimed that men didn't subscribe to her solipsistic feminist beliefs.

After her mother died, my ex-girlfriend ran away from Canada to teach English in Asia. She then partied through her twenties with many men there, came back at her epiphany phase in her late twenties, married a beta male that pined for her at 28 to fulfill her biological clock. Before promptly divorcing him at 38 when she deemed that he no longer served any purpose to her.

A popular video on my channel called '3 *Women Men Should Avoid Dating,*' was based on some women that I had dated that had:

1. Daddy issues,
2. Needed saving,
3. Fought with her children's father.

These types of women will never take ownership for their own lives. When I did that video on my channel, women with daddy issues sputtered their insecurities in the comment section. The example below is a typical response:

Pamela Rowles 2 hours ago (edited) 0 subscribers
so because my father decided to be a drug addict instead of a dad I am not worthy of a husband one day like it's my fault yea right u are truly a dumb prick like a man could of done what my mom did no man could ever compete with a mother like mine I don't need a man to tell me how I'm supposed to be treated instead I had a mom to teach me that I deserve the best and not to settle for some loser just to have a man around
Reply

Red flag #2 - Feminists

I briefly touched on this in the previous "daddy issues" red flag. Many western women today either identify as a feminist, or have welcomed toxic feminist beliefs into their schools of thought. They're indoctrinated to believe that men are privileged, that men hold women back, and that men succumb to the patriarchy.

Thankfully, the devout lifetime feminists are typically easy to spot. They:

- Avoid traditional feminine cues and instead opt for shorter, unnaturally dyed hair colors (think bright blue, purple, or red),
- Mutilate their body with several tattoos and/or facial piercings,
- Are often overweight and usually dress in ill-fitted clothes.

Versus keeping themselves fit, well dressed, and groomed to maintain their feminine physical appeal to men.

Feminism preaches radically leftist political views that fight for unlimited free abortion, elevate single mothers on a pedestal, and claim that masculinity is "Toxic."

Feminists hate it when the State imposes limits on abortion and tries to force them to be mothers. However, they more than happily use State family law to force men to be fathers.

Feminism teaches women to vote for the welfare state, massive government handouts, huge tax rates on top income earners, and social programs that widely benefit a female primary social order.

A feminist will never appreciate you or value you as a man. Feminism teaches women to be victims -   and anyone with a victim mindset can't find happiness.

Today's version of feminism is *so* toxic that it is anti-femininity. It encourages women to hate men, while simultaneously encouraging them to behave like men, and that they should ditch the notion of motherhood to prioritize their careers.

Feminism doesn't seek to make women better, or more feminine. Feminism seeks to make women into terrible versions of men.

Ownership is a concept that most women struggle with. However, feminists are often completely unfamiliar with it, and so everything will be the fault of the patriarchy.

Therefore, avoid *any* woman that identifies as a feminist - at all costs.

Since the #MeToo movement, we have seen several exceptional men fall to the false claims of sexual harassment or rape, and the vast majority of these false charges originated from feminist women.

Sadly, even feminine cues are not enough anymore. There are plenty of women out there that identify with feminist values that remain feminine in appearance, and these are the ones you must be the most careful with. As they are on a transformational path to obesity, collecting cats, and eventually short, brightly colored, hair.

If you are getting into an LTR, or are even considering marriage, it is *vital* that you give yourself a good two years to watch both her behavior and her choices in life. Pay close attention to her *before* you do something silly, like marrying a woman that appears feminine, but internally believes in feminist propaganda.

Red flag #3 - The unhappy and unlucky

Robert Green's tenth law states: "Avoid the unhappy and unlucky." If you haven't read *'The 48 Laws of Power'*, do yourself a favor and read it and always avoid the unhappy and unlucky.

And while this doesn't only apply to women, I note it here in this chapter as these types of women are a complete waste of your time. Their perpetual unhappiness will rob you of your joy.

Such women always have some problem going on in their life that attracts the "Captain Save-a-Hoe" type of guys to swoop in and rescue them from their own terrible existence and choices in life.

The unhappy and the unlucky often go from man to man, draining them of their joy and fortune. They are a magnet for drawing drama into their life - and yours. Therefore, only associate with the happy and lucky.

Red flag #4 - She competes with you

A woman that constantly tries to compete with you might seem cute at first, but it's a test of your competency as a man, and it's an underhanded behavior that ultimately aims to reduce your worth to her.

The female primary social order tells women that they are better than men, and it's why we see the rise of the "Boss girl" on social media. I once dated a woman that competed with her brother growing up, and that competitive behavior continued into her relationship with me.

It's a red flag because when women compete against you, she thinks she is better than you. A woman that thinks she is better than you *will not respect you* and will, ultimately, try to undermine you.

For a woman to satisfy her hypergamy, she must feel like she is with a man that, in her eyes, has at *least* 1-2 more Sexual Market Value (or, SMV) points than she does.

A woman won't try to compete with you when she believes your value is greater, she will instead admire you, and want to find ways to support your mission in life. Remember, women want to be with a giant. She *wants* to look up to you. Hypergamy never seeks its own level; hypergamy can only be satisfied if it does better than itself.

A woman constantly competing with her LTR, or husband, is *always* a prelude to a train wreck.

Red flag #5 - Keeps men from her past around

Women like to have options. A recent survey showed that almost half of all married women admitted to having a back-up (guy) plan. If you are getting into an LTR and she wants you to abandon your sexual strategy of unlimited access to unlimited women, then *she* needs to burn the ship on the shores of her new life with you and cut *all* emotional ties with other men.

Now, some women end up as an "Alpha Widow". An "Alpha Widow" is a woman who pines for that high value alpha that didn't commit to her in her earlier years.

She may not be in contact with him anymore. However, if she still sees him as the one that "got away" and she keeps a place for him in her head, and therefore her heart, then she *will never* see you as her best option.

It's imperative that she has a genuine, burning desire for you. You don't want to be "Good enough." You want to ensure that you are getting her very best.

Trust me when I say that no good ever comes from her having lunch with ex-boyfriends, or other male friends, and you *certainly* do not want to be the guy she "settled" for.

If you are a man that is chasing excellence in his life, then you don't need distractions like your woman seeking attention from, or still pining for, other men.

Men and women have little in the way of common interests; other than men wanting to have sex with women and women wanting to extract attention or resources from men.

There should be no room for male "friends" in her life if you are in an LTR. Women like this should be a plate, at least until they can prove that they are over their past. Nobody fucks more girlfriends and wives than "he's just a friend."

Red flag #6 - Poor with money

Some of you may know this already from my videos, but I'm well versed on financial services from my past businesses, and when women are bad with money, it's often serious trouble.

If she is an adult and doesn't have a pot to piss in or a window to throw it out of, then she is not to even be considered for an LTR. I've seen *far* too many men trying to play "Captain Save-a-Ho" and bail out women with horrendous debt and terrible spending habits.

Despite the lie feminism has told women that they only earn 75 cents for every dollar a man earns, women have every opportunity to earn a good living today.

Yet, women *still* continue to choose careers that pay *less* than men, while going into deep debt by overspending. Ultimately, if she can't manage her monthly cash flow and has nothing but a pile of handbags and shoe collection to show for her debt, avoid her for anything more than a FWB, because she will make *her* financial problems *your* problem.

Red flag #7 - Violent women

Women that have violent tendencies are a **massive** red flag. Early signs of violence are as small as a punch, or shove. However, I've counseled *many* men that have dodged knife attacks or even objects being thrown at them from their angry woman that was having a hissy fit.

Men are physically stronger than women, so when there is a domestic violence call into the police, even if you are the innocent party making the call, or defending yourself, it's likely that they will take you away in handcuffs, rather than her.

In most domestic violence cases, men are automatically presumed guilty and women are protected, even if she was the one starting the physical abuse. I've seen peaceful men, during a divorce, removed from their own home and children, because a violent woman accused her husband of domestic violence that never happened.

Violence from any woman towards you, for any reason, should **never ever** be tolerated, and is grounds for terminating the relationship immediately. To protect themselves, men **must** use their cell phone as a shield, and record a video of her erratic behavior as proof for the authorities.

If I haven't made my point clear enough yet - avoid all violent women **at all costs**! They aren't even worth a FWB arrangement! When it comes to violent women, the juice *truly* isn't worth the squeeze.

Red flag #8 - Extreme jealousy

Women want to be with a man that other women want to fuck. But they don't want their man actually going out fucking those other women.

This dichotomy of female nature is something that men will always struggle with. A degree of jealousy, also known as competition anxiety, is a good thing as it keeps her working hard to keep you. But it becomes undesirable when the women are *so* insecure in themselves that they always make her problems your problems, distracting you from your purpose.

They will be like a predator drone, always keeping watch on you. She will constantly text, scan through your receipts to see where you've been, what was ordered on the receipt, look for hairs that aren't hers, she'll want to look in your phone, creep on women that follow and like your social posts, and count the number of condoms in your nightstand drawer.

It's exhausting. She will drain you of your sanity, joy, and dignity. Jealous women have work to do on themselves, and it's honestly not your job to be their therapist.

Red Flag #9 - Party Girls

Most women under the age of 27 that have never been in an LTR are in their party years. If you met your girl in a nightclub, bar, or other social event, and she claims to be relationship material, but still continues to party several nights a week, you have two options:

1. Tell her that you don't date women who party without you and that if she continues, you'll wish her well and walk away.
2. Keep her in - but only as a plate.

The "party years" aren't exclusive to women under 28 either. Sometimes, she was married very young, had kids, and got divorced in her 30s and missed her "party years." So, it's not uncommon to see women in other stages of her life trying to relive that missed party era as an older woman.

You can't be in an exclusive LTR with a woman if she is going out partying with her friends regularly. The process involves two hours of preparation time in her hair, makeup, and clothes, for the main purpose of marketing herself to other men. If she is going out selling herself to others, she is not your woman.

Men have evolved to require fidelity from the woman they have invested time and resources into, as a step in ensuring paternity. This is not jealousy. Most men instinctively want to know that his woman is sexually exclusive with him.

Do not fall for the new age beta male narrative of polyamory. It is a mating strategy for weak beta men that must resign himself to sharing a woman with alpha men.

When there is a conflict between what she is saying and doing, and she is acting single when she goes out to party, then believe the action, never the words. Actions **always** speak louder than words.

I dated a few party girls, and their phones would always be going off at 2am from guys looking to hook up. Avoid party girls for LTRs and never limit yourself to one woman if you are dating a party girl. She simply isn't relationship material if she is out around other men, getting drunk or stoned dancing into the dark hours of the night.

Red Flag #10 - Heavily Tattooed and Pierced Women

I realize some men prefer women with some ink, and there will be men that will debate me on this. However, my experiences have taught me that their placement and frequency matters. One tattoo hidden in her bikini line isn't much to worry about, and probably bad judgement she regrets. However, if she has the classic "tramp stamp" on her lower back, or more than one visible tattoo while wearing normal clothing, then you might want to ask yourself what she is saying to the world.

Tattoos all over a beautiful woman is like putting bumper stickers all over a Lamborghini. You don't do it as it shows a lack of taste. I've never met a woman with several visible tattoos that didn't bring at least three or more red flags, mentioned in this chapter, to the table.

Heavily pierced women are another red flag. Draw the line at earrings, and if you want to push the limits, a nose ring. But, if that piercing is on her septum, nipple, clitoris, and eyebrow, or she even has multiple ear piercings up one ear, then keep in mind that you are dealing with someone that enjoys mutilating their own body, which is a red flag.

Red Flag #11 - Big Notch Counts

The most attractive quality in a woman is when you know she hasn't been with everybody and has her own standards.

Setting aside the higher probability of her having an STD, multiple conducted studies have proven that:

- The younger the age a woman loses her virginity at, and
- The higher the number of men she's slept with (AKA: Her notch count).

Often results in her being far less likely to bond monogamously to a man, in a healthy way, over a long period of time.

For example, a woman that lost her virginity at 14 and has slept with 30 men, is *far* less likely to bond monogamously to you over the long-term. Compare that to a woman who lost her virginity at 23 and has only slept with two men in long-term relationships.

If you want to get into a monogamous LTR, or take on the risk of marriage, then do it with a woman that's a virgin or with a low notch count that lost her virginity later on in life.

Research conducted by the Institute for Family Studies revealed that a virgin has a 5% chance of divorce after five years of marriage. Whereas, a woman with two previous partners has a 30% chance of divorce. The data stopped at 10 partners, which showed a 35% chance of divorce.

Promiscuous women that have had many partners and/or have been sexually active from a young age **DO NOT** make good long-term partners. It's not to say they can't, or won't, try to be a girlfriend or wife. But the statistics reveal how undesirable these women are long term, and that's why they should be treated as a FWB - and nothing more.

Women with a higher notch count are also more likely to report depression, become single mothers, have personality disorders, and have abortions compared to women with lower notch counts.

If you are dating a woman that has been with double digit or even worse, triple digit number of different men, then you are very likely going to be dealing with the baggage she is carrying around from all the other men that disappointed her, said mean things to her, may have physically abused her, or cheated on her. Women like this are brutal to deal with in a long-term relationship

Ultimately, women must preserve their value, while men must create theirs. It's why, throughout history, women's virginity was so prized. Whereas, a man's value comes from his ability to make something out of himself so he can provide, preside, and protect.

I should note that women will *never* reveal the truth about their notch count to you, so don't bother asking to get an authentic number. Some may volunteer it. Be wary of any number they throw out, as women often fear being slut shamed.

Women only usually factor in longer-term relationships as part of their notch count, and they often disregard all the one-night stands, threesomes, lesbian encounters, or FWB relationships that they had in the past. Short-term encounters are rarely accounted for.

At a bare minimum, double whatever number she gives you.

The lifestyle, and company a woman keeps, reflects her notch count. A woman that you meet at thirty that claims she was in an LTR from the time she lost her virginity at twenty-three, probably has a low notch count.

But women with an absence of a long term LTR in her past, that lived on her own, traveled a lot, and you met her at 35 could have a notch count approaching double to triple digits, or more. It's not uncommon for women in their party years (20-27) to rack up a notch count of 25 or more men.

Never forget, women become the average of the five people

she spends the most time with. If five of her friends are, or were promiscuous, then she will be the sixth.

Red Flag #12 - Single Mothers

Do not be a cuck. Do not raise another man's child.

There is absolutely nothing in it for you as a man. You do not pass on your own DNA; they do not have your last name, and cuckoldry shackles you with 100% of the responsibility as a parent, but with 0% of the authority.

Some men choose a FWB arrangement because it's low hanging fruit. However, I've dated single mothers when I was blue pilled and trust me: **DO NOT** DATE, LIVE WITH, OR MARRY SINGLE MOTHERS. It's not worth it. See the chapter on Single Mothers in this book for more details.

Look, I've counseled *hundreds* of men that have made the mistake of living with a single mother in such a way that the state views it as a marriage. Guess what? They have been on the hook to pay child support for kids they didn't even father.

In one case I counseled, a man was married for less than two years. He paid off over $100,000 of her debt and she brought two special needs kids to the table with her. She wanted out and was taking him to court for child support... for life.

Do not be a cuck.

Red Flag #13 - Women Seeking Validation

Social media is a staple in today's world, and almost all women are on it. However, women who use public social media to gain attention from men should be avoided. While there are no "good girls" on social media, the better ones will use private accounts. Meaning that only 'friends and family' can see their posts and they aren't posting provocative pictures, fishing for likes, comments, and direct messages from men providing loads of attention and validation.

Public accounts using social media to sell a product or service and treating it like a business are okay, but understand she will still have men flirting with her.

The women posting provocative pictures of themselves on public accounts on a daily basis, with thousands of thirsty beta males following them, are selling something too - their sexual agency. Women like this are openly optimizing their hypergamy.

If she is with you, but is still posting pictures for attention, then she is asking herself if *you* are the best that *she* can get.

Most women can become drunk on social media attention. So, if you consider an LTR with a woman that is constantly seeking attention online, then you need to continue to exercise your sexual strategy, and date her non-exclusively until she abandons her open hypergamy.

A woman's sexual strategy is open hypergamy, and when she is seeking attention online, she is out playing on the ice, trying to score a goal. Your sexual strategy as a man is unlimited access to unlimited women. Therefore, do not even *consider* monogamy until she abandons advertising herself. Do **not** take these women seriously. They are to be limited to plate or FWB status only.

Red Flag #14 - She Was a Sugar Baby, on Only Fans, or a Sex Worker

In a book by author B Rob titled 'Salty', the author shares his excursion into sugar dating as a "Salt Daddy". He also figured out how to identify if a woman has ever been looking for money in exchange for dating as a "sugar baby".

Ask some questions, and listen to her talk. Bring up the notion that you've heard about women using these sites, and ask her what she thinks.

You will need to search in her email for the term 'seeking' and see if there are any emails sent from the site in her past that show up. This will require that you look into her private life.

But, if you are looking for LTR material, then you need to take this step to ensure that you aren't going to make a whore a housewife. If she *was* a sugar baby, limit her to plate status only.

Red Flag #15 - Pathological Liars

Everyone, women included, lie. Many women, however, can't help but to lie pathologically. For some, their entire world is a house of cards, and they can't even tell when they are speaking the truth or not. These women are not LTR material, because they aren't trustworthy.

Fortunately, these types of women usually 'out' themselves over time because they can't keep up with their own bullshit. A girlfriend I had at nineteen lied about everything and anything.

I was riding sports bikes, and she told me early on how she had a sport bike at her mom's house an hour away. Although strangely, it was never available for her to ride, or she had it locked up in storage. There was always a story about how she rode, and enjoyed the experience, but always made excuses about where the bike was.

I was becoming suspicious of her stories. Knowing it cost me $9 to fill up the tank of my bike, I casually asked her how much it cost to top up her bike tank when she rode. She responded with $25. Right *there* I knew she was a pathological liar, and many of her other stories collapsed shortly after that.

Pathological liars are dangerous, they will tell you they are on birth control, when they aren't, they will lie about things that will put you, or your health, at risk. If you are attentive and poke at her stories, then these women are simple to spot.

Red Flag #16 - Baby Rabies

This is an interesting term I came across after I got divorced and re-entered the dating pool around 39. I had this annoying feeling that most of the childless women in the dating pool were desperate to get married and have children. Some of them were so thirsty to get married and have kids, that they would even ask if that's what I wanted before asking me anything else.

Sometimes it was even in their opening message on a dating application. It felt like they were looking for a dutiful beta with sufficient provisioning ability, and decent genes to settle down with.

Women exhibiting desperation to get married and reproduce are not into you and will not support your mission. They will not complement your life, but will instead want to be the focus of your life.

Any woman attempting to rush you into having kids and getting married, without allowing for a two-year vetting period, is a big red flag.

But, if you feel that you are simply an accessory to fulfilling her biological imperative to reproduce, or that she is counting her eggs every month, as they dry up? She has baby rabies.

Move on and don't let her problems become your problem. She either earns it, or can go become another man's problem.

Many of these women put degrees and careers ahead of their prime child-bearing years. As they approach their mid-thirties, they grow desperate. Remember, men can capably father healthy children well into their fifties. For women, their prime childbearing years decrease rapidly after the age of 30.

Red Flag #17 - Hissy Fits

Some women never learned the social maturity required to process their emotions, so they resort to hissy fits to deal with their differences in a relationship.

When my daughter was 3-years old, if something didn't go her way, she threw herself on the ground, face down, then kicked and punched with her limbs at the ground while screaming. This is the toddler version, and it's excusable in a child, because they don't know how to process their emotions with maturity when something doesn't work out for them, so they start kicking and screaming.

In an adult woman, hissy fits are an unacceptable red flag and come in many forms.

Rather than approaching the issue head on like an adult, she might start by passive aggressively going on social media to post something revealing and sexy, behave erratically, or make underhanded posts about you.

One says, "Hey fellas, I'm over here, and my man pissed me off; look at me and shower me with validation and attention." The other is a passive aggressive maneuver to shame or ridicule you, usually with some covert statement or meme.

Hissy fits cover a wide range, including but aren't limited to overtly stating something like: "Just leave my shit on the front porch" when things aren't going their way. Or using actions like hiring a male personal trainer you know she was intimate with in her past, and posting a picture on social media of themselves together, with some trite caption about how, "This girl will get her body back," in an effort to push your buttons.

These outbursts by women are bad news, and I've noticed that there is often a correlation between her hissy fits and daddy issues. I've seen fathers set logical, responsible and reasonable boundaries for their daughters to preserve her value as a woman, and she would routinely break them in a rebellious and dangerous way in protest.

For example, a traditional European father will often set limits on when his daughters can date, and in what cultures he sees as a good fit for the family. A woman with daddy issues that can't respect the boundaries set by a man will go out, and throw a hissy fit by seeking out, then intentionally have plenty of dangerous sex with men from cultures that she knows her father would be vehemently opposed to. Even if it resulted in an STD, or an abortion.

Deal with hissy fits head on, and treat them as unacceptable behavior, otherwise you will constantly deal with them in your relationship.

Also, **do not** argue with women. They will not let a thing like logic or reason get in the way of their emotional hissy fit. You set the boundary, then cut off all contact (called a "soft next") with her for about four to five days to let her think about it.

Remember, attention is the coin of the realm for women, so when you remove it, they start to lose their mind and will usually automatically fall back in line. She will either comply, or it's "Goodbye."

Most women, because of their own solipsistic nature, will not recognize it as a "hissy fit," even if you spell it out for them. So, be resolute. You will get out of life what you tolerate. **Do not** argue with her about her hissy fit.

Look, men are deductive, rational thinkers - women aren't. Therefore, a soft next allows you to return to the table with a boundary you set. If she doesn't like it? Show her the door.

Your front door should always be unlocked if she wants to leave, but locked if she tries to return without fixing her hissy fit issue.

A woman that has a genuine, burning desire for you, and is serious about sorting herself out, *will* do the work. A woman that isn't, will resist, gaslight you, make excuses, and will *constantly* test your boundaries as a man.

Red Flag #18 - Be in Control of Birth

As a man today, once your sperm leaves your balls, women make 100% of the decisions unilaterally and as a consequence of that, she can make your life a living hell..

If you knock up the wrong woman, you could be on the hook for around 20-years as her personal ATM. NEVER, **EVER** trust a woman you are not in a properly vetted LTR with when she says, "It's okay, just go inside me, I can't get pregnant." You must have **100% certainty** that there is effective birth control in play. Oh, and for the record, birth control pills are *not* sufficient.

Many men have knocked up women who claimed to be on the birth control pill, only to discover she "accidentally" forgot to take them or wasn't even on them. Condoms (that *you* flush away afterwards), a vasectomy, or an IUD, are your most reliable methods of birth control today. Remember, women lie. It's called birth control for a reason, always be in control of it.

Red Flag #19 - Drama Queens

All, not some, women periodically crave for some form of drama. If they are bored, and there are no issues in your relationship, they will manufacture indignation to test you and create those "feels". Drama queens choose random molehills to turn into mountains. This is also another form of a hissy fit.

I guarantee you will encounter drama with a woman at some point. But, if it appears more than once within the first three months of dating, or more than a weekly "thing" during your LTR, then she is flat out telling you that this drama will be a regular occurrence for life.

Buckle up buddy, you'll be in for a roller coaster ride if you don't put your foot down and use a "soft next" to maintain boundaries.

Manufactured indignation is really just a shit test, and it's also about testing your frame as the dominant frame in a relationship. Remember, drama *will* happen with *all* women at some point. So decide early on what you will, and more importantly what you won't, tolerate. Alpha men with plenty of options will tolerate very little to no drama, lesser men with few options will accept it as it comes.

Red Flag #20 - Addictions

Dependency to things, activities, or substances is a big red flag. Women that rely on alcohol, shopping, drugs, social media, cigarettes, news, or reality TV to name some examples, can be highly problematic to a man that is chasing excellence in his life.

Unhealthy addictions, if left unchecked, will dominate her life, her choices, and her conversations. Addicts, usually, become self-destructive. If it's negatively affecting your life, then it has become an unhealthy addiction.

A woman who is addicted to a reality TV show will talk about the mindless drama between characters on the show non-stop. Alcoholics are always looking for their next drink, and anyone that's ever dated a woman that's addicted to antidepressants knows how badly it affects her body weight, mood, and sex drive.

Don't let women make her addictive problems, your problems. Smart men do not get into an LTR with women that have addictions, it's **not** your job to save, or cure them.

If they have acknowledged their addiction, and are working on their problems with a professional, good, let them. But keep her at arm's length as a plate until she has shown genuine progress for several months. Also, make sure that her addictive personality doesn't replace one addiction with another.

Red Flag #21 - She Can't Be Led

Of course you must be a man capable of leading in a relationship, but in our current "Boss Girl" era, women today are more disagreeable than ever. Most women today believe that men don't want a feminine complement to his life that is pleasant and agreeable. Toxic feminism has convinced women that a man today wants to be challenged by their strong and fiercely independent woman. These women cannot be led - no matter your frame or SMV.

She will argue with you over trivial things and constantly test your frame as a man. This can lead to contempt, and if she starts name calling, eye rolling, mocking she is going to look down on you. Contempt is the No.1 predictor to the end of your relationship.

If you are a strong and unplugged man, a woman that can't be led will make your life miserable and steal your joy. Look out for obvious soundbites or hashtags in her social media posts like #bossbabe #bossgirl #girlboss or #badbitch. Boss girls might be fun to date casually, with their playful jabs, but in a LTR, a strong man wants an agreeable and pleasant woman, not a disagreeable and bossy one.

Conclusion

As I stated earlier, you can ignore my warnings about these red flags, and get involved with these women. But, at some point, your life *will* become complicated and unnecessarily difficult.

As a man, it is incumbent on you to shoulder the burden of performance and to chase excellence. In life, women can either become an anchor, or a sail. Look for women that are a complement to your life and that gladly fill your sails with wind and limit your interactions with anchors that hold you back from your mission.

The cold hard truth

Never forget:

- It's *your* responsibility to set, and *always* enforce, the boundaries that are meaningful to you.
- Never date, LTR, or wife-up a single mum. Neither the mother, nor the kids, will *ever* truly appreciate you for your sacrifices.
- If a woman *ever* becomes physically violent with you, then you **must** get the hell out of that relationship immediately. And if you have kids with her, then see an attorney ASAP.
- If your spidey senses are tingling and your gut is telling you something, then there's a reason why. Listen to it.

- A man who's chasing excellence and making his dent in the universe will have the options and self-respect to drop *any* woman who's complicating his life.

Steve From Accounting's's Field Report

Well, where to begin? I originally edited this chapter in the midst of a "less than amicable" divorce, from a "boss bitch" Doctor who waved her - many, many - red flags right in my face over our 16-years together (10-years married with two young kids together), but I was too much of a zombified, thoroughly plugged-in man-child to see them.

I ignored her culture (her parents were originally from somewhere in Asia) and she rebelled **hard** against their more traditional cultural norms as she was born in England. Her family dynamics were screwed up to say the least, and I didn't even know what boundaries were to have any.

It's clear that I failed to take note of the **abundance** of red flags that were openly being waved in front of me because I didn't know they were even red flags to begin with.

However, after I ended our marriage by telling her it was over (there's only so many chances you can give a pathological liar when you have kids together before you need to take what little self-respect you have left and leave), it was a good 18-months before I'd squared away enough of my own shit to get back out to begin dating again.

Suffice to say that the dating market (at least via the online dating apps) is a veritable dumpster fire of every red flag noted here - and more (across every major dating app).

I still vividly remember my *very* first date with a new woman since separating from my (now ex) wife. She was 10-years younger than me, fit, flirty, and was down for some same-day fun. "Awesome!" I thought.

We went back to hers and then the biggest red flags started piling up from there. First was the fact that she wanted me to choke her about 30-minutes into it all. While this was new to me (I was with my ex-wife for 16-years and never did this), I worked my way through it as confidently as I could.

What transpired over the next few, increasingly intense, hook-ups were a myriad of additional red flags with it culminating in the fourth time visiting her house. I'd made us dinner at hers and I - inadvertently - mentioned I had kids (I deliberately kept them out of my dating profile as I was only looking for something casual - so they'd never meet my kids, so no need to know as far as I was concerned).

She looked shocked and upset and tried turning on the waterworks. She asked me to leave, so I said "Sure, I understand" and I immediately went to put on my shoes to leave. She stopped crying and looked surprised asking if I was really leaving. **Major** red flag clocked right there. She then began to tell me a tale of how she punched a man who lied to her before and she had a glint of satisfaction in her eyes as she showed me what she did to him.

It was then that Rich's 7th Red Flag suddenly popped right into my head, mentally recalling it verbatim. I immediately got up, wished her well, but told her that I won't see anyone who intentionally punched a man just because "he lied to her." I had her blocked on WhatsApp and on my phone before I'd even left her house.

In my earlier plugged-in days, where my scarcity mentality was real, I would have more than likely ignored something like this as the sex was - to be frank - *leaps and bounds* better that what I had with my ex-wife (which I appreciate is easy to say after no sex for the prior 18-months). I believe "Crazy in the bed; crazy in the head" is the saying.

However, I'd taken to heart the content of this book (and I'd also been casually seeing other women at the same time), so I had enough self-respect to GTFO of there without a second thought.

While certain red flags cited here may have some nuances to them for you to factor into whether or not *you* let them into your life at all (a call only you can make yourself), the **vast** majority of them should be non-negotiable for an easier and more peaceful life.

Thanks to this book and Rich's community, I learned to value my most important resource: my time. And I'm now **substantially** more protective of it. That doesn't mean I don't slip up on occasions. But, I am now able to reflect on that, see where I messed up, and make sure I don't make the same mistake(s) again.

If you find your life becoming "complicated," it's because **you've** allowed it to become so (and then tried to justify it to yourself afterwards). Be more conscious of your choices in life and you'll find it's no coincidence that your success with women will improve ten-fold.

13

GETTING "DA GIRLS" ONLINE

It's exceptionally important for me to open this chapter by stating that women should never be the focus of a man's life. Chasing excellence, finding purpose, becoming competent in all realms of life, making bank, and self-care need to trump chasing tail. Every. Single. Time.

Remember, beautiful women are not a scarce resource. High value men that have their lives sorted out are the scarce resource on the sexual marketplace, not beautiful women.

The cold hard truth about online dating

Now that we've gotten that out of the way, understand that when you use online dating apps, the deck is always stacked up against you if you aren't in the top 20% of men.

Several dating sites have released data over the years on how men and women use online dating sites. And some startling results have emerged confirming what the red pill has been saying for decades.

The top 78% of women are competing for the attention of the top 20% of men. While the bottom 80% of men are competing for the bottom 22% of women.

Confirming the reality of women's hypergamous nature on dating apps.

What that means is, if you are a high value man (so an 8/10 or better), you are spoiled for choice with women on dating apps. It's absurd to say this, but a 3/10 female is shooting for the 8/10 male or better - and she'll genuinely think she's in with a chance of landing one.

If you are a 7/10 male or lower, you are basically competing for scraps. So, again, this is why it's vital for men to understand that chasing excellence, and not women, will always be your best ROI in life.

Dating sites and apps are filled with overly entitled and bratty women. Many possess an over-inflated sense of self-worth and, to top it all off, the vast majority of them are single mothers with many of them trying to sell that you raising *their* kids is them bringing value to the relationship.

How to assess your value

I'm a big fan of getting an ROI on every area of life. So, knowing now how women use dating apps, we can approach it from an informed angle, giving us better results. This is a two-step process.

The first step is a brutally honest self-assessment. Take a good, hard, look at yourself and your life, and rate yourself on a scale of 1 to 10. With 10 being the absolute best version of yourself, and 1 being the worst. **Do not** compare yourself to a Hollywood actor, or a billionaire. You are asking yourself: "Am I the best version of myself?"

Factor in the following for your age: Your job, wealth, self-care, your physique, look, style, your network, your hobbies, if you have kids, how compelling you are, your car, and your home. The "Seven spokes of a high value man" chapter covers most of this.

These areas matter to women, so be completely honest with yourself.

Now that you've rated yourself, go onto your dating application of choice, and set yourself up to see what the female experience is like in your age range and location, but set it to "Female seeking Male."

You are now looking at your competition. This will help you understand what you are up against. Now use this newfound knowledge of your competition to make a correction of your sexual market value assessment - if you require it.

If you are a 6/10 or lower, then I'd discourage you from using dating apps. Instead, I'd encourage you to double-down on yourself and do the work needed to increase your value on the sexual marketplace.

If you are a 7/10, you're going to have a harder time. Therefore, good photography can be an equalizer to improve the optics of your value one point higher. However, don't rely on trick photography, you still have work to do.

If you are an 8/10 or higher, then congratulations, you've done *some* of the work. Continue to keep working on yourself and enjoy being one of the 20% of men that are spoilt for choice on dating apps.

How to get results

There's three parts to doing well with online game (after that, everything happens in real-life):

1. Photography.
2. Bio.
3. Messaging.

PHOTOGRAPHY

Photography is arguably the most important part. On matching apps like Tinder or Bumble, it's the primary driver that dictates in which direction she will swipe. It's also the area where you can create the illusion of a SMV that's one to two points higher if you do it right.

It's essential that you hire a photographer to take pictures for dating apps or social proof.

There is an oversupply of young photographers that you can hire for a few hundred dollars on your local classifieds, for two hours to do a professional photo shoot.

To get the most out of it, bring three different, but well-fitted, outfits, and ask the photographer to select some suitable locations that they are familiar with shooting at. Make sure you show up looking sharp with a fresh haircut and let them work their magic. Many men have significantly improved their results with women on dating apps with the correct use of superior quality photography.

Once you've got your collection of eye-catching photos, the next step is to use a site where real women rate your pictures for dating purposes.

At the time of writing this book, Photofeeler is the best platform available to get genuine feedback from real women.

How to level-up your photos

Once you've narrowed down your top three professional photographs (based on the top three ratings from a rating site), you can stop there if you like. However, it often helps to include the following three additional compositions into your profile. These are: The "group of friends" picture, the "mystery" picture, and the "Aww!" picture.

The "group of friends" picture is straightforward and is designed to immediately establish high value through social proof. You'll get bonus points if your circle of friends looks successful, established, and they look like the type of people and social circle that she wants to be around.

You are basically telling her, "Hey sexy, if you date me, you'll get to know these legends and hang around my people." For example, a group photograph on a yacht will always do better for you than a group picture in a trailer park, surrounded by lower-value men. So be intentional when selecting a "group of friends" picture. This is another reason why it's incredibly important to surround yourself with winners in life.

The mystery picture is one of my favorites, because it caffeinates the hamster in her head, and runs her imagination wild. This is always a solo picture and it's best taken at sunrise or sunset with the light behind you, and your image as a back-lit silhouette.

The following photo of me is a solid example and was taken at sunrise at a resort in Mexico. It works well because you can clearly see my physique, the 'V taper' and because I was enjoying a natural moment in the pool. The fact that I am also half naked will get her mind racing to manufacture ideas.

Give her something mysterious to think about.

The "Aww!" picture is something that will pull on her heartstrings a bit and should ideally be a picture of you with a pet. It doesn't need to be your pet, but cute puppies are, by far, the best accessory for this picture.

Stay away from cats, or a kid (even if they aren't your kids). The only time I would suggest kids for this type of picture is if you are building a school on a Caribbean island after a hurricane (and you're surrounded by kids that obviously aren't yours).

Even if you are a single father, I'd still discourage you from posting pictures of you with your kids. Like it or not, women are inherently solipsistic, and are self-interested in what they can benefit from being with you. If you signal in a photo to potential women that you are a father with kids in tow, it's highly unlikely to benefit you. Women don't think to themselves, 'oh I can't wait to raise another woman's children' so save those details for a later time.

Your biography

The biography (or bio) section is far less important than the pictures. But it's still worth covering from the perspective of what not to do.

Do not drone on and use the full character allowance. Truthfully, she doesn't even care that much, and she has already made 98% of her decision about matching with you based on the pictures she has seen. The point of the bio is to caffeinate the hamster in her mind that bit further and get her really curious about you.

We know women are hypergamous and solipsistic. So, all your bio needs to convey is that you are her best option (of the many available to her), and that there's something in it for her.

My typical bio would read:

> 6'2", successful entrepreneur putting a dent in the universe. Great social circle of friends and adventurer, looking for a feminine beauty to join me.

That's it, that's all you need. It says I'm tall, make bank, have an impressive network, and that I am not boring. The bit about "putting a dent in the universe" should get her asking questions if she has a strong interest in you. The "join me" bit lets her know right off the bat; she's entering *my* frame.

With women, you can do almost anything you want to them - but do *not* bore them.

Some guys will use clever lines like: "Like my shirt, it's made out of boyfriend material." And while that may seem smart, truthfully, it comes off a bit desperate. Make women qualify for *your* time - not the other way around.

Messaging

So, you've got matches; now let's talk about messaging. The vast majority of men get messaging totally wrong. The **entire** point of communicating back and forth on a dating application is to weed out the manipulative time wasters and then get her number to set up a date.

That's it. The biggest mistake men make is in wasting time "getting to know her." That's not what she wants. Nor do you want to waste your time chatting up someone that looks nothing like their pictures, only to be disappointed in person. If you are a 8/10 man or better, she wants to meet you.

Keep in mind, many women will use dating apps just to get fleeting social validation from men. They will ignore, or ghost, any guy they have low desire for, even if they previously matched with you.

Your first message to her should be something playful like: "You look like you could be trouble."

Ask this question to establish her interest level. A woman with a high level of interest will respond, and engage with you, preferably with a question about why you said that, bring some playful banter, or ask about your awesome pictures.

If she isn't asking questions, uses noticeably brief responses, or takes a long time to respond, she isn't that into you.

If she asks questions, be somewhat vague in your response. Remember, you want her qualifying herself to you, so be curious. Women love exciting and mysterious men, so don't show up and verbally throw up all your most interesting information before you even meet her.

For me, women try to establish what kind of entrepreneur I am, or businesses I run. Not because she is interested in the business, but to establish how much I earn running it. She might ask about my business, or what dent I am putting in the universe. To which I would often reply with: "I'm a board advisor in a national financial services business, real estate investor, and do my own private equity investing." All true, but most women won't understand what any of that means, aside from I'm important, and again, that I make bank.

After I drop that bomb, I'd often follow up with: "So what do you do?" Not because I particularly care, but to subconsciously establish that my SMV is higher than hers.

Once you've exchanged a few messages back and forth, message her with: "I'm busy today, and I'm not on here often, but what's your number? Let's set up a date to meet soon."

If she is into you, she will give you her number. If not, she will give you an excuse. It's always one or the other. The medium is the message, gentlemen.

Also, do not take her social media as a replacement for a phone number. GET. HER. PHONE NUMBER! Women want a man that can take control and set up the date and you need a number to do that.

If she offers you to follow her on social media, immediately decline the offer. She wants you to be one of her hundreds of thirsty betas orbiting around her there, giving social validation and free attention to her. You are on a dating app to date, not become her twelve thousandth one hundred and fifty first follower on social media.

If she says she barely knows you and wants to chat more on the application, tell her you are a busy guy, and only on there to date in real life. You're not there to accumulate pen pals. Women that say this do not have genuine burning desire for you, she only sees you as an alternative if her line of other, more preferable, options don't work out.

Again, if she has a genuine desire for you, then she **will** give you her number. When she does, text her within a day, and set up a date. Otherwise, unmatch her and move right on.

The date aka: "The sniff test"

Your first date with her should be an hour or less, and nothing more than a drink or coffee. The whole point of the sniff test is to:

1. See if she is worth your time.
2. Determine if she has a genuine interest in you.

The total cost shouldn't be that much. You always pay and do not split the bill for a drink - you will look like a loser. My preferred first date would be to grab a coffee and then go for a stroll in some public space like a park or hiking trail.

You want her to feel comfortable. However, you also want to get a good look at her since most women today use older photography, filters, or even touch up their pictures, so they rarely look better in person.

If it's during the day, meet her at a coffee shop, grab your drinks, and then find your way to an outdoor trail. If it's at night, make plans after eight for a drink so she isn't expecting a free dinner, and then chat her up on a patio or bar.

If she is unfamiliar with the area for a date, send her a Google map link for the location so she can find it with no trouble. You lead, and set the location for the date, not her.

Unless you are in her area on business or travel, always have her meet you halfway. The more she has to travel, and the less you need to, is preferable for you for two reasons:

1. It saves you time.
2. It tests her for genuine burning desire.

A woman with a strong desire for you will drive two hours

to your house on a first date. She'll then gladly drop to her knees at the door without saying a word (on your instructions) and give you the best blow job of your life.

Trust me. **Do not** go running to her front door for dates. If she insists that you travel to her, then she is telling you right off the bat that she doesn't have that genuine burning desire for you and only sees you as an option, not a priority.

Each new meeting should start by standing up with a big smile, including a brief handshake, or if you're so inclined and comfortable, pull her in for a brief hug. Then, gesture to either sit, if it's a night venue, or stand in the ordering line if you are getting coffee and going out.

Some hardcore pick up artists like to aggressively go for a same day lay. And, while you may be successful sometimes, my preference is to just do a "sniff test" on her. Just to see if she is even worth seeing again and to check if there is a genuine connection there or not.

When the hour is up, walk her to her car, Uber or transit and, if you have a connection, bring her in for a hug, and/or brief kiss and let her know you'll be in touch. If there is no connection, just say your farewells and leave it at that. You don't owe her an explanation.

Getting laid and spinning those plates

Women today are more promiscuous than any other time in history. Sexual intimacy should happen by the second to third date for three reasons:

1. You make it clear that you have a genuine interest in her sexual attention and are not interested in just being a friend.
2. You want to ensure there is a good sexual connection.
3. Sex is awesome.

Some guys might argue that it's too soon, or they will wait "for the right girl". Unless she is clearly from a good family, and a virgin, I'm here to tell you that this is the wrong way to approach it. Never forget: **Women break rules for alphas and make them for betas**.

If a woman is happy to have sex with the hot dude from the foam cannon party in Ibiza 15-minutes after she meets him, why should you wait eight dates?

Unless you are Amish, all of today's modern women on dating apps have hooked up with many guys prior, so don't think for a minute she is the Virgin Mary.

Some people like to argue that there are "good girls" you should wait to be intimate with. The truth is, the only difference between good girls and bad girls is: Good girls just haven't been caught yet.

The best way to facilitate sexual intimacy is to begin with your messages leading up to the next date. Make it clear you are interested in her sexual attention. It's men that play the "nice guy" that get "friend-zoned" by women, earning them nothing but non-sexual attention.

When women have genuine desire, they will send you provocative pictures without request. Other times you will need to request them. Other women may not send naughty photos at all, but will openly engage in some naughty talk with you. Don't act desperate, but sub communicate that you crave her. Either way, it should be crystal clear to her after the first date, aka: "The sniff test," that you are interested in her sexual attention, and it should be mutual.

If it's not, and she wants to "get to know you first" because she has rules, remember that women break rules for alpha men, and make them for betas. You will never get her "best" if she sees you as a beta, but she will give her best to Chad Thundercock on the first date. My view is never date a woman if she treats you as a beta as she will always hold out on you.

Ideally, set your sex date for an evening, and host her at your place. If she drinks, have a selection of wine or vodka at your house. If you don't have your own place, you will need to go to her place. Or, if you're a younger man and still with your parents, skip the drinking, and having a car with tinted windows is always useful.

To get to sex, you need to get comfortable and confident with escalation. Music is great for setting the mood, I use whatever sexy playlist off is trending on a popular music app. You can escalate the sexual tension by inviting her for a hot tub or sauna if you have one, or you can simply start by touching, and kissing. If she reciprocates warmly, then escalate, and move to heavier petting, which should lead to sex.

Always be in control of birth

As a man, you must **always** be in control of the birth. Once your sperm leaves your body, *you no longer have any decision-making ability to terminate a pregnancy*. The government will force you to pay child support - even if you don't want the child.

All control is now with the woman. So **always** have condoms on hand; do not "raw dawg" a woman (no matter how horny you are). You cannot rely on her promise of being disease free, or on reliable birth control. Women lie, and they lie *often*.

You should also have a "Plan B" on hand in the event a condom breaks. "Plan B", more commonly known as the morning after pill, is effective. It's an oral tablet she takes, which very quickly triggers her period, removing the risk of your sperm fertilizing her egg. These single tablets are usually bought at the pharmacists counter, you just ask for it.

If you have an accident, make sure she takes the morning after pill in front of you, and you **know** for sure that she swallowed it. Women have been known to take them in the bathroom with the door shut, and just spit it into the toilet or garbage if they want your seed bad enough.

Again, I **cannot** put enough emphasis on this; **<u>always</u>** be in control of birth, do **not** rely on a woman's word. As the old saying goes, an ounce of prevention is worth a pound of the cure.

If you get involved on a longer-term basis with her, and are getting fed up with condoms, then you may want to consider other forms of birth control, like an IUD. However, I **strongly** discourage you from ever trusting her to take a birth control pill - or any other oral contraceptive.

"Surprise" pregnancies often come out of her forgetting, or intentionally not taking her birth control. IUDs are generally considered more than 99% effective, and you cannot 'forget' to take your IUD, it's always there..

There are male birth control pills going through clinical trials at the time of writing this book, and the studies reveal that they work by compromising your testosterone levels to make your sperm ineffective. **NEVER** use this form of male contraception! You will become weak, unattractive, and feminized. It's a pill that basically turns you into an old infertile man. Either have her on an IUD, use condoms, or get a vasectomy if you have absolutely zero interest in children.

The cold hard truth

Never forget:

- 80% of women are only interested in the top 20% of men online. The other 80% of men who are invisible to them are left fighting for the bottom 20% of the super-low SMV women.
- Be completely honest with your own personal value and mark it accordingly. Put your focus into developing these areas *before* you re-enter the sexual marketplace.
- Stand out from the crowd by investing in some professional photography. Seriously. It'll pay dividends - trust me on this one.
- Texting is mostly for logistics. By all means, open

up with something fun and flirty for her to bounce off of. Once she's asking questions, get her agreeing to a date ASAP.

- Don't be single-minded in trying to get laid on the first date. It's more important to vet her for potentially serious red flags (such as seeing how she responds if you tell her "No." with a smile on your face). *Never* stick your dick in crazy.

- Finally, **ALWAYS** be in control of the birth. **Without exception**. Far, *far*, too many men have been already duped by women with "baby rabies". **Do not** let yourself become one of them.

Steve From Accounting's Field Report

As someone who came out of a 16-year relationship (which, ironically, started via the Yahoo dating site back in 2004), entering the world of dating apps today was very... insightful (to say the least).

I'd deliberately stayed away from dating for 18-months after I separated from my ex-wife as I thought it was critical to work on my own shit first (many thanks to Rich for the focus on chasing excellence over women).

My ex-wife was taking our kids away on their first foreign trip away without me, so I decided to make the most of those two weeks without my kids by hitting every major dating app at the same time. Keep in mind that I'm 5ft 6" and I have a No. 1 buzz cut all over. Granted, I'm in the best shape of my life (and I dress far better now to highlight my improved physique), but I'm *definitely* no 6ft Giga-Chad.

I - very quickly - learned a few hard lessons about not wasting your time writing bio-focused openers in an effort to impress the woman.

Instead, I curated an opener that works very well - for me. I simply ask them if they have an allergic reaction to my type of accent, followed by a winky emoticon. It's a unique opener, my phone has it saved in auto-type now, and it *immediately* allows me to vet for those women who:

1. Have a sense of humor.
2. Reveal just *how much* they like my type of accent (a desire barometer if you will).

I can then riff off of her response with an aim to get her number within 10 messages to set up a date.

I also hired a professional photographer and went into London for the photoshoot. I then found some photos taken of me at some sporting events I attended and put the best ones up for rating.

I then picked the best ranking "action/competency" shot (me leading the race pack during a sporting event with a huge smile on my face), I added a few more, and then tweaked Rich's own intro message to suit me and my personality more.

I think it's fair to say that I managed to prove to myself that I was *clearly* in the top 20% of men locally, as I not only had a sufficient number of matches, but I had the entirety of those two weeks chock-full of dates with many different women (some with two dates on the same day).

However, let me be upfront and honest here. I wasn't sleeping with 9/10 Swedish supermodels (but I also swiped left on 90-95% of the profiles I saw - so I only swiped right on the women who I thought looked genuinely attractive).

I quickly came to accept that the local dating market where I am dictated what my options are (by the responses I received) and I welcomed the opportunity to sharpen my skills both in - and out - of the bedroom, and to also take that data as proof that I still have work to do if I want to attract the "9s and 10s". Which is a win/win as far as I'm concerned.

I also very quickly learned to take rejections *as a good thing* (versus taking them personally). When I was ghosted, or the match flaked, I internally thanked them for respecting my time by taking themselves out of the equation early. Ghosting, flaking, all that shit happens. It's literally a part of modern day dating.

It's your job to have such a strong, **genuine** abundance mindset that it doesn't get to you one bit. You need to be able to just shrug your shoulders and keep on chasing excellence - regardless of who ghosts, or who ends up in your bed.

Shit, having a scarcity mindset is *truly* toxic (and, looking back, was the main reason why I chose who I married). Do **everything** you can to maintain an abundance mindset when it comes to every aspect in your life, and you'll find that your mental and emotional health will *truly* reap the benefits.

After a year or so of using the main apps, I had more than my fill of crazy bedroom antics with numerous different women. I even had to let several women go because they wanted more than I was willing to offer them (or because they were trying to withhold sex in return for exclusivity - I immediately showed those women the door). My vision of how I want to live my life as a free man is **absolute**.

Keep in mind that, if you're single and you're - genuinely - working your ass off to improve every area of your life (even if it's just one day at a time), you'll soon start to stand out from the sea of simps and men who are too lazy to do *any* sort of work. And I truly do mean that.

I remember seeing the Tinder profile of the **very** first woman I went on a date with from the apps (see the 21 Red Flags chapter for how *that* escapade ended!). I was curious to see what the local competition was like, so I watched as she showed me her profile with over 1,300 likes. And another 25 came in - in real time - while we were both looking at it (at 2am on a Saturday morning).

The profiles of my "competition" was - to be blunt - fucking atrocious. Shit photos aplenty, overweight, fuck-all style, and an inability to even hold a basic conversation that was even *remotely* stimulating. She openly acknowledged that she didn't have the time to open even a fraction of those likes, and of the ones she did, barely any appealed to her at all.

As things currently stand, the only dating app I bother with right now is Facebook dating as that offers less BS (and a better quality of woman) where I live in the UK. However, I have 100% confidence in my ability to jump back onto a different dating app (or two) and line up a number of dates within a day or two.

In this day and age, men who are chasing excellence and can sub-communicate this through a well-presented dating profile (and who can also hold an engaging conversation online), are a **very** rare commodity. Like, *insanely* rare.

Ignore the doomsayers who say you "must be over 6ft" to date women online. I've had ONE woman openly state that she wouldn't date me because of my height (via a dating app). ONE. I'm 5ft 6" and effectively bald. And yet, I can go online today and get dates (and get laid) if I wanted to. Because I'm doing the fucking work to make my whole life better. And women can see the value in what you're sub-communicating to them with how you carry yourself.

You won't click with everyone. That's OK. You'll be Ghosted. That's also OK. Keep working on yourself, improve your profile with Rich's tips, and learn from any mistakes. It truly *does* work.

14

SINGLE MOTHERS

In the 21 Red Flags chapter, I covered several warning signs that men should be aware of with women. However, this book wouldn't offer a useful roadmap for men unless I cover the *why* part. I'll explain why a relationship with a single mother often invites both drama, and unnecessary complexity, into a man's life.

I've had well over a thousand coaching calls with men, and the one common denominator that keeps repeatedly showing up is that men dramatically complicate their lives by inviting single mothers into them.

Now, not every single mother is bad news. But, the reality is, they bring a lot of problems into men's lives that women without children simply don't.

When I got divorced at 39, after seven years with the same woman, I had shared custody of my small child, and I did what most men typically did in that scenario. I looked around and found that most women in my age range had children in tow.

Most had several kids, and sometimes, each kid came from a different father.

I got involved with a single mother almost immediately. She was also recently divorced, pretty, fit, knew how to cook, she also had the typical post-divorce breast augmentation, and she had two kids in tow that were seven and ten when I met them. If you want to learn more about my personal experience, search YouTube for "entrepreneurs in cars and why men shouldn't date single mothers."

Some men would argue from experience that there are dozens of problems that come from relationships with single mothers. However, I'm only going to focus on the five I've seen most often.

They are, in no particular order:

- Cuckoldry,
- Responsibility without authority,
- The victim mindset,
- Financial issues,
- And re-prioritization.

Cuckoldry

When you take on the financial, parental, and emotional burden of raising another man's children, you are, by definition, a cuckold. Some men would argue that if she is a widow, or he was a deadbeat father that disappeared from their lives, there is an exception. Well, there isn't.

Regardless of how you want to rationalize it in your head - you are still a cuck.

Society today encourages and celebrates cuckoldry. You'll often see articles titled: "The case for being a cuck." The truth is, it's nothing to celebrate.

They don't take on your last name, and they definitely don't possess your genetic legacy to pass down. These two points have historically been the biggest selling points to men for fatherhood. For most men, this is enough to enforce a firm "pass" rule on single mothers. But, many men still ignore the obvious problem and it is because they lack better options because of their own limited values and beliefs.

To add insult to injury, women overwhelmingly get awarded primary parenting of their children the *vast* majority of the time, while men don't. So, if you are a divorced father, then you might end up spending more time parenting, raising, and investing resources into the children of another man rather than your own.

Responsibility without authority

Getting involved with a single mother often means that you will find yourself in a position where you have the same parental responsibilities as a biological father, but with none of the authority of a parent.

Shortly after she introduces you to her kids, she will expect you to "step up" and take on parenting duties.

It often starts with going out for dinner, and she brings her kids along for the first time. This is when you will be expected to demonstrate that you can provide for Billy and Bobby too. You'll be on the hook with parental responsibility for birthdays, travel, holidays, ski trips, teaching masculine skills, the beach, the list goes on.

You will fill the shoes of "Daddy" and your financial resources will certainly be warmly welcomed. But, at some point during a grievance, you will also eventually hear them say something like: "You are not my father! You can't tell ME what to do!"

They will be "our" kids when she needs you. However, they'll be "her" kids when you need to discipline them or enforce healthy boundaries.

Strangely, if you are a single father, you will learn that when your kids need something, your children are never "ours," but selectively "yours." Yet, most men discover that women want authority over his kids, just without the responsibility that goes along with it.

Most men eventually hear her say something that reflects the mindset of: "Not my monkey, not my circus." There is a reason why some kids that grew up with a stepmother call her "Step-monster."

If the fact that you are being cucked as a man isn't enough to make you question your choice to get involved with a single mother, then expect to have responsibility, but with zero authority. Whereas, she will often take on little responsibility herself, while still seeking authority.

The victim mindset

Women are naturally solipsistic (after all, it is hard-wired into them). However, single mothers run a special gauntlet of mental gymnastics that they rationalize as normal. But, ultimately, it boils down to them adopting a victim mindset.

They often brag on social media about how they are strong, independent, and "don't need no man." While simultaneously turning to the government for handouts, and/or their children's father(s) for financial support.

I dated a lot of single mothers that would complain about the father of their children and often heard her use disparaging terms like: Loser, dumb, deadbeat, beta, or boring. If I would ask them why they married him, or had kids with him, their face would turn to stone as if to say, "How dare you hold me accountable for my own choices."

Naturally, she didn't own her choices. She was always pointing and sputtering at her ex-husband, her boss, her father, or the President. With the rare exception, she rarely looked in the mirror to take ownership for her results in life.

While I've only ever dated traditionally feminine looking women, I've never met a single mother that wasn't a feminist.

To identify as a feminist, you must have an oppressor and, when it comes to feminist logic, every woman is oppressed by default and is therefore a victim.

The victim mindset requires her to be unhappy, unlucky, and oppressed. When I started dating these women, I found out first-hand how hard done by she claimed she and her children were, and it was always someone else's fault.

Her children also adopt this mindset (because kids naturally learn their behaviors from their parents). So, if something doesn't go their way, they will emotionally manipulate their mother, and have her side with their bratty behavior. Even if you were right and they required boundary enforcement and discipline.

Most men love playing the role of "Captain Save-a-Hoe." And, since most single mom's love being a damsel in distress, men are all too happy to step-up, and swoop in to protect "her honor."

Financial issues

When it comes to money, women choose jobs that pay less than men the vast majority of the time. Even though there are more women in the workforce than ever before, men earn the vast majority of wealth by choosing higher paying professions. Most men discover that single mothers gravitate to professions like: Nursing, Teaching, Dental Hygienist, Daycare Work, and Hairdressing.

Few women, especially moms, take on difficult jobs with long hours that pay over six figures. So, when I was dating them, I found it difficult to meet a single mom that earned as much as I did.

For the most part, they aren't driving modern cars with a warranty or living in mortgage-free homes.

Most single mothers have debt, problems and often, also have nothing to their name (except the children in tow with another man's last name attached to them).

You will be called upon to pay for her life and that of her children's. I've had several coaching calls with men where they paid off her debts, bought her kid's cars, and paid for their college tuition. It's common for plugged in men to make themselves less, so she and her children can become more.

Reprioritization

In general, men are all too happy to abandon their purpose in life to fulfill a woman's. Unfortunately, when you get involved with a single mother, you will never be her priority.

Most men find their place in a pecking order behind: Her needs, her kid's needs, her work issues, her wine drinking nights with her "sisters," her salsa nights out, and then her cat.

If you get involved with a single mother, it's highly unlikely you will ever be anywhere near the top of her priorities.

You will often be expected to make your hobbies and passions less of a priority, so she can focus on hers. There's an old soundbite that calls women "Dream killers." The truth is, most men that get into relationships with single mothers will be required to shift their priorities around for her and her kids.

The BIG risk

There is an often-overlooked risk with dating a single mother, especially if you have a young daughter, and she has one or more boys. The biggest risk to young girls is being physically violated through non-blood related relatives in the household. This is far more common with girls, but it does happen to boys too.

There is hard wiring in our DNA, as a function of survival and for genetic diversity, to avoid sexual activity with blood related relatives. It's why brothers and sisters are sexually repelled by one another.

There are many women out there today as a consequence of the higher divorce rates, that have been raped, or sexually assaulted, by stepbrothers or stepfathers during their childhood.

This is a risk that you need to be aware of if you are a divorced dad, more-so if your ex-wife isn't particularly good at picking men. If she invites characters into your daughter's life, with stepbrothers in tow, then you must find a way to have that rational conversation with your children's mother.

When dating a single mother - *might* - make sense

I've often been challenged to present a situation where dating a single mother might make sense. I can only think of one.

You've already got children, so you've secured your family name and DNA. Her child is about the same age and sex as yours, so they can interact and relate with one another and, most importantly, there is no risk of her being violated.

Your frame also naturally infers 100% authority in the relationship. She isn't a feminist, and takes ownership for her life, and holds her kids accountable to your standards. She is, at a minimum, financially equal to you. She is a complement to your life, and certainly not the focus. She'd also have to be attractive, have a genuine burning desire for you, and also get on well with your child.

To be perfectly honest, I think you'd have much better luck finding a Leprechaun with a pot of gold at the end of a rainbow, than finding someone who can comfortably meet every condition. So, my advice to single dads, especially if you are a high value man, is to focus on women without children.

The cold hard truth

Never forget:

- You don't want to be a cuck. You might genuinely love her kids "Like they're your own." But, ultimately, they will never ever be yours and your bloodline will not continue if you don't already have kids.
- They'll never, ever, ever respect you in the way that you want them to. Even if you adopted them. Because, deep down in their core, they'll always know that you "Aren't their father."
- While it's a cold truth that a woman's kids will always be a higher priority than you, with single

mothers, you'll be even further down in her list of priorities. Until she wants something from you that is.

- The victim mindset, along with unhealthy doses of shaming and guilt-tripping, is the de-facto method-of- operation for single mothers. If it's all the bio father's fault, and she can't own up to anything that she did to screw up the relationship, then you can bet your ass she'd say the same about you to the next guy.
- The vast majority of sexual violations are perpetrated by close family members. If you have a young daughter, then it's incumbent on you to make sure she stays as safe as possible and make sure she feels comfortable enough to tell you anything. So lay the groundwork in making her feel comfortable enough to confide in you ASAP.

Steve From Accounting's Field Report

The vast majority of the women I've (very) casually dated have been single mothers. However, I make it *crystal clear* from the outset that I will *never* meet their child(ren) and neither will they ever get to meet mine. If they don't like that, I wish them well, and then move on with my life.

Granted, these women who I've been seeing casually have been matched with on various dating apps in my area. I tend to find more women who *don't* have kids when I'm out doing something I'm passionate about (which, for me, seems to be at nightclubs, at national endurance events, or at salsa dancing lessons/parties).

This is (one of) the main reasons why the main woman I've been dating (the one I mention on a few occasions who has the genuine burning desire for me) *won't* become an LTR with me. It's just simply a dynamic that I don't want to add into my life and she completely understands *and* respects that.

I will stick my hand up at the fact that, early on, I picked the "low hanging fruit" online and had plenty of fun with many different divorced single mothers, as it allowed me to sharpen my dating and conversation skills, my game, and my bedroom skills while I leveled my life back up post-divorce.

However, I only did so because I **knew** that my boundaries and frame were now **cast iron**. I'd spent the years working on my own shit so I didn't repeat the same piss-poor choices that I'd made in the past.

However, if *you're* still squaring away your own shit mentally and emotionally (and be 100% honest with yourself on this), then *stay well away* from even casually dating single moms. They **will** try to lock you down if you tick their boxes (aka: hypergamy) and you **cannot** waver from your own frame or boundaries for all the reasons Rich has listed in this chapter.

And, as someone who was adopted, as much as I respect and appreciate my adoptive father for taking my sister and I on legally when we were kids, the cold, hard, truth is that I cannot love him in the same way I can my mother - my relationship to each one is **completely** different.

Keep this in mind if you find your "Captain Save-a-Hoe" senses start tingling around any "unicorn" of a single mother you find yourself crossing paths with. Her kids **will not** love you in the way you *want* to be loved (and the same goes for the mother herself).

If she's fit, feminine, and she wants to *genuinely* compliment your life then, by all means define a solid "FWB" style arrangement *that works for you*, and be ready to let her go (gently) when she - inevitably - develops feelings for you and wants to lock you down.

Know that day **will** come and wish her well in her life. And, if you don't ever meet her kid(s), then you can't form any attachment to them either. This seems cold, but it's in the best interests of **everyone** involved. Trust me on this one.

With regards to the safety aspect, as someone with a

daughter and an ex-wife who has recently introduced our kids to her new partner's kids (he has a son the same age as mine and a younger daughter), I'll be upfront and say that I've been having to push through a **lot** of anxiety with this as my ex-wife *point-blank* refuses to let me meet her new partner (so I can see what his character as a man is like).

It was one of the key reasons why I never left my ex-wife sooner than I did - the fear of another non-blood relative man (who is a stranger to all of us) being around my kids. My daughter has just started puberty, so I've had to keep on top of reminding her to "take her privacy seriously." I've been reinforcing the same ethos with my son.

However, I can only trust and hope that my ex-wife hasn't picked someone with a proclivity towards young kids.

Bottom line, Rich's advice is here for a reason - and I absolutely follow it now that I'm free once again. There's *more* than enough guys out there who are only too happy to take on another man's kid. Cool. Let him take on that responsibility (but without any real authority).

You'll find that the quality of the options that come into *your* orbit will naturally begin to increase as you continue to focus on increasing your own qualities as a man. Like with MGTOW/going "Monk Mode," by all means have a bit of *temporary* fun when you're there, just don't stay there permanently. Future you will thank you for it.

WHY SMART MEN AVOID MARRIAGE

Let me start by stating I'm not opposed to marriage or having a family. We are just a slightly higher form of primate, and make no mistake - as men, we're designed to scatter and pass down our seed. It is in our biological imperative.

I am, however, against allowing the state to decide what happens to your wealth, your freedom, and your access to your children if a marriage doesn't work out and inviting a woman into your life that has more red flags than a Chinese communist parade.

The divorce statistics vary slightly around the world. But, on a balance of probabilities, about half of all marriages end in divorce within seven years. Remember, this statistic ignores the other half of the men who are usually either living in an unhappy, or sexless, marriage.

In a study by Acevedo and Aron on both romantic love and long-term relationships[1], they discovered that only 13% of their participants, in an average of an 8.39-year relationship, felt "romantic love". And only 2% felt "obsession" for each other.

Meaning the comforting lie (about living in a state of bliss for eternity), isn't real and in a failed marriage, as the legal contract becomes untied, it's the male (and not the female) who is most often the one who is left in ruins. With him picking up the pieces after the couple goes through the relentless grind of the divorce machine, before being spit out the other side.

Throughout history, men have always been the disposable sex, and women the protected sex. So, it would make sense that everything in family law today favors the woman, while being hostile towards men.

It's time to drop some cold hard truth bombs about the reality of marriage in today's Western world, and the bottom line is this:

> "Marriage is a high reward/low risk choice for women, but a low reward/high risk choice for men."
> - *Richard Cooper*

I should clarify in this chapter that, when I say, "Western family law," I am including almost all First World, modern countries indoctrinated by today's version of feminism.

Throughout most of history, men were at the head of the household. They were legally responsible for the actions of their spouse and children and could keep order in their home by more or less whatever means they saw fit. If a man's home was his castle, then everyone within was his vassals.

We don't know exactly when and where the tables began to turn. But things started changing in the late 1800s when the state passed new laws. For example, in 1895, London passed a bylaw prohibiting wife beating past 9pm. However, this wasn't originally designed to   protect women. It was primarily a noise pollution issue in the densely populated city.

In the book *A History of Marriage*, by Stephanie Coontz, she concluded that, for tens of thousands of years, people married not for love, but for the acquisition of in-laws, assets, and influence. Church records, personal diaries, and public court records showed love wasn't even part of the equation.

Men had 100% authority, and 100% responsibility to the

family unit. Family and their in-laws took care of medical care, law enforcement, the elderly, schooling, and so on. Men were the head of the household, and there was little to no state involvement in how a man ran his family.

This was a time when masculine virtues were both respected - and valued. But, in the last one-hundred-and-fifty-years, a toxic version of progressive feminism has changed it all. Toxic feminism has reversed the roles so both women and the state are now at the head of the household.

Today's men no longer have much authority in their house, yet they still have 100% of the responsibility. Almost all authority has been taken away from men and has been given to both the government and women, while men maintain all the financial responsibility.

What is even more troubling is that, with the recent #metoo era, something as fundamental as establishing the facts first is no longer required. Instead, we are to believe all women when they accuse men by default, no questions asked.

Family law

When I was getting divorced in Canada, I thought I knew what the process would look like. But, truthfully, I had no idea what I was up against. I approached divorce with a naive eye, viewing it as a simple process with a fair exit for everyone. Every expectation I had was way off.

In fact, I was *dead wrong*.

Within the first hour I talked to my family lawyer, he had dropped so many truth bombs on me that I walked away from the call with a feeling of complete hopelessness. I actually believed I'd be lucky to see my daughter ever again. That I'd spend the rest of my life bending at the knee to the state and my ex-wife. While I simply watched as my wealth left me, and as I also became alienated from my child.

I'll never forget my lawyer's words: "If you have the penis, and go to court, you are going to lose - and badly." I was shocked.

Hadn't feminism leveled the playing field for women? Aren't women equal to men?

If so, then why am I being told that, because I was born with a penis, I would lose by default in family court?

They say the original intent of progressive changes to family law was to deal with deadbeat dads who didn't look after their kids, right? Well, it did, and then it kept going on, becoming a supremacist movement against men which hasn't ever stopped.

In today's world, women are the supreme rulers in both the household and in family law when untying the knot. Western governments designed every part of legislation to preserve and improve the mother's interests, while simultaneously destroying the fathers. In Western family law, for one gender (the female) to advance its cause, it comes at the expense of the other gender (the male).

If you are considering marriage, then the best thing you can do is buy one hour of a local family lawyer's time. Sit down, listen well, and learn how the law handles men in your state or province. Because there's a 50% or more chance your marriage will end in divorce.

Remember, this divorce statistic doesn't take into account the people who remain married because they are too unattractive, broke, and lack the option to leave. Or simply because they are cowards.

It is nearly impossible to calculate the number of unhappy marriages that persist.

Domestic violence charges - A woman's trump card

Domestic violence charges, alleged by the mother against the father, is a trump card which has been built into Western family law. Men can be forcibly removed from their own homes by the police for false or exaggerated claims of domestic violence. It also includes being alienated from their children, while the courts enforce unreasonable payments to the mother from the father. In turn, restraining you from entering the house you paid for, or accessing the children you fathered.

I had a coaching call once with a man who was cheated on by his wife several times. So, he decided he'd had enough, and that it was time to divorce her. During the acrimonious separation period, he became upset with her one day and pointed a finger at her face and angrily proclaimed, "You are a fucking liar."

The finger-pointing was enough for her to call the police, make a claim of domestic violence, and have the authorities involved. There was no violence, no physical contact, nothing.

Just an angry finger being pointed while saying five words.

It's absolutely vital that you always keep in mind the following phrase: The woman you marry is never the same woman you divorce.

Remember, Western family law is written in such a way that it assumes women are the weaker sex. Men are the privileged sex and are also the abusive sex by default.

How women behave during divorce

Men need to understand that through a combination of family law and female nature, women are motivated to behave incredibly poorly to the father of their children during the divorce.

There are significant female-centric financial rewards that have been written into family law encouraging women to be the sole custodial parent of the children. By becoming the parent that has primary custody of the children, money, and all decision- making capacity, goes to the parent awarded custody. Which, eight times out of 10, is the woman.

Let's be clear about something. Women are opportunistic by nature, it's hard-wired into them, and it's part of the reason why sapiens are such a successful species. Without opportunism, her children were less likely to survive. You can't blame women for this; opportunism is an evolved survival mechanism.

Women needed this skill to find the best provisioning mate, and to optimize their hypergamy. If you give someone, that's naturally opportunistic, incentive to benefit at another's expense then, guess what, they will do it.

It's only in recent history that female opportunism has had the full backing of the state behind it as family law. Interestingly, prior to the last 150-years or so, if there was a divorce, then the father would most often get custody of the children and retain all family assets - including what she brought to the table.

Once a parent has custodial rights, they can make unilateral decisions without the other parents' consent. Even if that decision is not agreed upon by both parents.

Depending on where the law governs your divorce, that could include choices about school, extra-curricular programs, religion, medical procedures, and even where the custodial parent chooses to live.

The financial rewards are not exactly small either. There are three major financial drains from the parent that isn't the custodial parent:

Alimony

Also known as maintenance, this is the first level of responsibility that a man must pay to his ex-wife if he was the breadwinner in the home, and she didn't work, or earns significantly less. For some men, that was because she was a stay-at-home mom. For others, she just never worked after the marriage, and there were no kids.

Either way, you are responsible to upkeep her standard of living after the marriage ends. The monthly cost, and duration of the payments, depends on where you live, and how long you were married. In some places, like California for example, if you are married for 10-years or more, then it's lifelong alimony.

Child Support

Child support is paid to the custodial parent to cover the cost of raising the children. Contrary to popular belief, the payment amount is not based on what the children actually need to survive. Rather, it's based on state issued tables. I had a friend who calculated   that, during his marriage, the monthly cost to look after his child for things like food and clothing were around $500 per month.

The state issued child support tables, however, compelled him to make a legally enforceable payment of $4,367 every month. Child support, for the most part, goes to the mother, not the kids and has nothing to do with what your children's needs are.

Editor's Note: For those of you living in the UK, search online for the "Child Poverty Action Group (CPAG) Child Support Handbook (2022/2023 edition). It costs £45, but it's *very* well written, easy to read, and is very insightful in this area. It's well worth the small investment (just be ready to swallow some very bitter pills as you read through it).

Matrimonial assets

Assets accrued during the marriage are divided after the knot is untied, usually 50/50 in most cases. Although, there are places where *more than half* of the assets can be awarded to the mother. So, every asset you acquired, before, or after, the day you signed that contract with your government go into one pile, and it's then potentially split it down the middle, *regardless of who paid for it.*

In some cases, a prenuptial agreement may protect assets that were acquired before the wedding. But, if circumstances changed during the time you were married, or a considerable length of time has passed since the prenup was signed, then a judge will most likely throw out your prenup and it won't be worth the paper it's written on.

Since men rarely stay home to raise children, and women are hypergamous in their mate selection strategies, then you can begin to see how unlikely it is for the mother to pay the toll of family law. For the vast majority of cases, it's the men that are left in financial ruin. With little to no access to his children, watching helplessly as his money flow to his ex-wife, while she alienates him from his kids.

Hypergamy doesn't care if she vows to love and be with you "In richer or poorer, in sickness or in health... 'til death do us part."

Divorce, and not career or entrepreneurship is, statistically, still the number one-way women acquire their wealth today.

For a clear example of this, as I write this chapter in a Starbucks, a woman at the next table said to her girlfriend, complaining about her husband. She said: "I can divorce him, take half his shit, the kids, the house, and not need to put up with his dumb ass anymore."

That, gentlemen, is the world that this toxic version of feminism has created.

How the state encourages women to become single mothers

In the spring of 2019, angry single mother journalists from around the world attacked me for warning men on Twitter about the dangers of getting into relationships with single mothers. They manufactured about a dozen hit pieces, all from a three-minute clip of a 50-minute speech that I gave an audience of men.

You can watch my video response by searching "The truth sounds like hate, to single moms that hate the truth" on my channel for more perspective.

An overwhelming show of support came from men, and some women, praising me for shining a light on this unflattering subject. However, a golden nugget appeared from commenter "Kim Brown" in the comment section of the video, she said:

> *"The thing that infuriates me is my hubby makes about $50,000 per year, I make about half that. But when you are talking to people about taking responsibility for themselves, you do realize that if I were to leave my hubby and become a single mother with government benefits, I'd have way more money. What we pay in taxes as a couple, opposed to what the government would give me if I was on my own isn't even close. So, when women leave there [sic] husbands they are improving their situation until that changes nothing else will. It's sickening when society rewards those who make bad choices!"*

She went on to expand on that with the following:

> *"My friend, who is a single mother, does the same job and makes the same money as me. We sat down and compared our finances and, with all the subsidies and tax breaks she receives from the government, she has about $1,000 a month more than my family in disposable income. To me, that's not just rewarding single mothers, it is actively punishing middle to low-income women for staying with the father of their children."*

If there is a more damning piece of evidence that the state is encouraging women to leave their marriage and become a single mother... Well, I'm not sure where to find it.

Arguments for marriage

Some men might argue that their girlfriend is a "God fearing religious woman." Or that his beautiful fiancée comes from a home with conservative values where both of her parents remained happily married for twenty-years.

That isn't enough, for two simple reasons:

1. A woman always reserves the right to change her mind at any time.
2. Even conservative, God loving religious women will leverage the corrupt family legal system to benefit from family law.

I had a coaching consultation once where a man spent a good part of the call framing what was to become the "evolution" of "her" during his marriage. She went from a church going religious woman from an unbroken home, to someone he didn't even recognize during the divorce process.

It shocked him that she had performed a 180-degree pivot during the divorce. She filed a false domestic violence charge to get him out of the house. Allowing her to control the sale of the home, obtain primary custodial caregiving, and earn maximum benefits from the child support tables.

I simply cannot endorse marriage in its current state today.

But Rich, don't men have an obligation to find a "good girl" and settle down?

No, you don't. However, men *do* have an obligation to become the best possible version of themselves. If a woman enters your frame, is a complement to your life (but not the focus), and you want children, then - and only then - should you consider having children (after a proper two-year vetting period).

But you must always remember... Women always reserve the right to change her mind.

All you need to do is browse the divorce discussion forums

for 10-minutes to see loads of women who think that, just because the child came out of their body, that they are the sole owner of that child. Therefore, they are entitled to be the primary caregiver by default.

Better yet, spend an afternoon sitting in on divorce hearings at your local family court, and see with your own eyes how fathers get treated.

Societal conditioning, media, feminism, and the law all reinforce that men are inept clowns, incapable of being a useful parent to a child. Fathers are, however, useful as tax cattle, so the state can milk and then transfer those assets to a mother.

Society celebrates single mothers so much that, during Father's Day, you will see memes being passed around that are praising single mothers for doing the job of both parents. However, single fathers receive no praise on Mother's Day.

For more on this topic of the feminization of society, search for a video on my channel titled 'Why are today's men so feminized?'.

Throughout history, men were valued. However, with the state at the head of the household, we have slowly been reduced to that of the disposable parent and are treated like tax cattle. Fathers are no longer the head of the household, the state is. The state ensures that women are well looked after. Even if it comes at the father's expense.

It's absolutely essential to understand: "The woman you marry is not the same woman you divorce." Mark my words - a woman's true colors will come to light in a divorce.

For one side to advance its agenda it will come at the cost of the other. Win-win scenarios in divorce are rare because of female hypergamy and only sometimes happens if a woman marries a man of lower value than her (which is even rarer).

Understand that women are not natural risk takers, men are. Now, wrap your head around the fact that women initiate about 80% of all divorces, and often plan them months, or sometimes years, in advance. They do this because they are confident that they will do well - because the state makes sure of it.

Remember that taking unnecessary risks is not inherent in female nature because women play not to lose. It's men that play to win.

Also, men, if you were caught cheating on her, always understand that hell hath no fury like a woman scorned. Female nature is not on your side. It expects *you* to forgive *her*, to look past *her* indiscretions and, in many cases, it expects you to take full ownership for the reason(s) why *she betrayed you*.

Divorce and suicide

It was a warm spring day as I drove along the freeway. I was six months into my separation, and still living in the matrimonial home trying to hash out the details of my divorce. I was driving into the office in my truck, feeling utterly depressed about how things were going for me.

This was when overwhelming thoughts of suicide entered my mind. I felt powerless, and the notion of taking off my seatbelt, flooring the truck, and quickly slamming into a concrete pillar entered my mind. I figured it would be over fast.

It was easily the lowest point in my life. My life was out of control, and I had no idea if I was going to survive financially, or even see my daughter grow up.

Throughout history, men have been conditioned to be tough and to "man up." We fight in horrible wars and do incredibly dangerous jobs that women aren't typically willing to do, like work in mines, or on oil rigs. But when it comes to the emotional and economic toll of divorce, simply put, men can't cope very well. Divorced men are also more than twice as likely to commit suicide as married men, and divorced men are almost 10 times more likely to kill themselves than divorced women.

Unfortunately, this is something that the mainstream media won't shine a spotlight on. Remember, men are disposable; women are protected.

Children and divorce

Even in today's modern world where women are working, and have income equality, mothers are still awarded a "primary caregiver" custody order about 80% of the time. That usually means that the father sees his child(ren) every other weekend and a Wednesday night - for dinner only.

My family lawyer said this is par for the course, and it's often called the "Screw over daddy deal."

Women often argue, "Children need their mothers," and family law still sides with that notion. Which, of course, is utter nonsense. Children need access to both of their parents if they are going to be an effective member of society as an adult.

Approximately 43% of children in North America are raised by the mother. Here's some more statistics that men should know when relying on the mother to raise their children:

Fatherless boys and girls are:

- Twice as likely to drop out of high school, twice as likely to end up in jail, and are four times more likely to need help for emotional or behavioral problems. [2]
- 85% of youths in prisons grew up in a fatherless home. [3]
- 85% of children who exhibit behavioral disorders come from fatherless homes. [4]
- 71% of pregnant teenagers lack a father. [5]
- 63% of youth suicides are from fatherless homes (five times the average). [6]

Mothers, by an overwhelming margin, are doing most of child rearing post-divorce. And, despite how single mothers are praised in the media for being strong and independent, they're often doing a terrible job at it.

How marriage changes men

A lot of men I've coached through divorce entered the marriage with some beliefs they came to learn weren't true. And most of those men were downright shocked by what happened to them.

Men's testosterone levels decrease

It's been proven that when a man lives with a woman, and has children, his testosterone levels drop. Some would argue that this process is just andropause, and natural. But unmarried men of the same age usually have higher testosterone levels than their married counterparts.

Paternity fraud

While it's difficult to get reliable statistics on this (because of gynocentric laws in some Western countries that lean towards no paternity testing), it's estimated that somewhere between 10 and 30% of married men are raising children that aren't biologically theirs.

This is a big issue because - one of the bigger selling points of marriage to most men - is the ability to pass down his seed. Marriage is, in theory anyway, supposed to protect paternity.

Betatization by a thousand concessions

Women will constantly test a man's frame. The vast majority of men will go through the slow process of agreeing to his wife's endless requests and demands. It often starts with "Honey, put your dark clothes in the dark hamper, and your white clothes in the light hamper." Before progressing on to "Let's go vegan together," and may eventually escalate to "Let's have a poly relationship." Which inevitably ends in a speech about how she "Loves you, but isn't in love with you."

Throughout your marriage, the question isn't if you will be

betatized. It's more of by how much and will it be to the point that you become so unattractive to her; she leaves. It's important to note that women don't do this intentionally, it's just a natural part of female nature alongside the societal conditioning of the sexes.

Reduced sex drive

Men often marry under the impression their wife will reward them with the reliable, consistent, and wild sex that they had before they got married. Yet, one of the biggest search queries from married men is: "How do I get my wife to fuck me?" or "is masturbation when married considered cheating?"

Sexless marriages are extremely common today. Introducing kids into the relationship will dramatically change the dynamic between both of you, her sexual availability, and her enthusiasm for you. Another, often overlooked reason for this, is that her competition anxiety drops considerably when she lives with you. She also subconsciously knows family law has her back.

She knows where you are at all times and where you live. Therefore, the competition anxiety that she had when you were both living under separate roofs would keep the hamster between her ears caffeinated. With her constantly wondering what you might be up to.

For more information on competition anxiety search "Entrepreneurs in cars what is competition anxiety."

How to minimize the risks of marriage

I've had men propose all kinds of ways to eliminate the risk of divorce rape, from importing foreign brides, to surrogacy. Look, there is no way to remove all risk. But, from my research, I've discovered a few things that you can do to minimize it:

Live where shared custody is the default arrangement in divorce

There are a few places around the world where, upon divorce, both parents share custody 50/50 by default. Unless one parent can prove that the other parent is a risk to the children's safety. So, if one parent is a heroin addict, with a history of violence, or criminal activity, then there may be an argument for a sole custody hearing. However, be sure to ask a family lawyer in your country about this.

Have both a pre-nuptial and post-nuptial agreement

A prenuptial isn't enough, and many people will tell you they really aren't worth the paper they're written on during a divorce. This is especially true if 10 years have passed since you got married and she stayed home to raise three kids while you worked. They just have less value over time.

However, there are cases where judges have enforced a prenuptial, because a postnuptial was signed after the marriage, thereby confirming the original terms. You must remember, any nuptial agreement loses value over time. As circumstances change again, be sure to ask a family lawyer in your country about the best way to handle this. You must protect your assets.

Don't marry down (too far)

Men typically marry down. It's not uncommon for the VP of Accounting, who's making $360,000 a year, to marry a hairdresser that's earning just above the poverty line. When you marry down, she doesn't return to her hairdresser lifestyle upon divorce. It is you who'll be expected to maintain the lifestyle she became accustomed to in the marriage.

Family law doesn't allow women to return to the poverty line, especially if there are children in the equation. Therefore, if you choose to marry in a Western country, then find someone that brings similar assets to the table. Or ideally someone who earns as much, or more, than you (although even that brings its own unique set of problems in a divorce).

Don't marry a Feminist

Feminism teaches women they don't need men, that we men are disposable. How men have oppressed women, why men are the privileged sex, and that women are better than men. You simply cannot expect a woman to stick around when they subscribe to a belief system that indoctrinates women into simultaneously being a victim and a supremacist, all while hating the opposite sex.

Seek the "bright triad" traits

They are:

1. Clarity,
2. Stability,
3. Maturity.

My friend Dr. Shawn T. Smith, author of the book 'The Tactical Guide to Women,' would consider a woman who displayed these traits as being a high-quality woman. Read this book, then read it again, and seek out these traits.

Avoid the "dark triad" traits

They are:

1. Narcissism,
2. Machiavellianism,
3. Psychopathy.

Narcissists are easy to spot today; she is the woman that is constantly seeking attention on social media throughout the day.
Machiavellianism is when a person is so focused on their

own interests that they will manipulate, deceive, and exploit others to achieve their goals.

Psychopathy is traditionally a personality disorder that is characterized by persistent antisocial behavior, impaired empathy and remorse, and bold, dis-inhibited, and egotistical traits. It is sometimes considered synonymous with sociopathy.

Although it's not specified in the dark triad, I would add Borderline Personality Disorder (or BPD) to this list of traits to avoid.

Wait two years before you marry

Dr. Shawn T. Smith pointed out that women can put on an act, *especially* if they are post-wall and in a rush to get married due to "baby rabies."

Therefore, be sure to "Hire slow and fire fast." Do your due diligence and take your time vetting a woman. One of the biggest complaints that men who marry too quickly have, is they learn that they were merely dating a representative of the woman. And that the nice representative leaves after she says, "I do." If, by the two-year mark, it's not a "Hell Yeah!" then it's definitely a "Fuck no!"

Live together

You'll only see someone's true colors when you live with them. Live with them for at least six months to see if you still like them on the seventh month. Also, don't listen to people that tell you that marriages have a higher chance of failure if you live together before you marry. This is true in North America by a tiny percentage point. But, in Europe, most marriages fare better where a couple lives together first.

See how she handles stress

Flight got canceled? Her baggage was lost? Sandra at the

office is a royal bitch every day? See how she handles stressful situations, and if she can make the best of them. Stress happens in marriage, so dealing with stress maturely is a skill needed for a successful marriage. Avoid a woman that can't handle stress, or one that makes mountains out of molehills.

She has a good relationship with her father

I'm assuming you are a masculine man, or one seeking that level of excellence. How can you expect a woman to admire, and look up to you, if she didn't have a positive masculine male role model in her life growing up? See my chapter "**21** Red Flags" in this book, as I cover "Daddy Issues" extensively there.

She takes your last name

We live in a world today where some women, usually feminists, won't take on your last name. Sometimes, I've heard of weak beta men taking on their wife's last name. In an environment where the burden of all risks is on the man's shoulders, your wife should take on your last name. And, no, hyphenation isn't acceptable either.

It shows that she is in it for the long haul and is willingly entering your frame. There are some cases where women with a professional designation, for example, a Lawyer or a Doctor, can't change their surnames without a substantial amount of hassle. But, as far as the marriage license, passport, driver's license, etc., then her last name should change to yours.

Don't complicate the wedding

Do not get involved in the long, drawn-out process that is wedding planning. Photographers, videographers, band, DJ, limo, venue, meal plan, invitations, and so on. If you let yourself get carried away in the planning, then you will overspend on something that already has a 50% chance of failure.

Therefore, keep it simple, have a justice of the peace perform it or, even better, make it fun and have a destination wedding. Statistics also show that more expensive weddings have a higher probability of divorce. A woman that is in your frame and admires you will not insist on a giant party that's all about her.

Conclusion

Marriage is utterly unnecessary in today's day and age. It is all risk for men, and all reward for women. If you want to have children, then my advice is to leave any Western country, state, or province that is hostile towards men. Instead, live somewhere where there's ideally no alimony, no division of assets, and no child support to worry about.

There are still feminine women that frown upon feminism and value masculinity. Find one of these women and live where the law isn't going to destroy you.

The cold hard truth

Never forget:

- The woman you marry, will not be the same woman that you divorce. A woman's true character will be revealed during a divorce. So, don't be surprised if she makes up loads of crazy stories to get family law, and potentially even the police, to do her dirty work for her.
- If you have kids with her, then be ready for her to weaponize them during the divorce. She'll do absolutely everything in her power to turn them against you and alienate them from you. Rest assured, that this will test your personal resolve and frame to the absolute limit. Being alienated from their kids is one of the biggest reasons why so many

men either commit suicide, or at the very least, contemplate it.

- If you've been betatized by a thousand concessions, and you begin to take back your life and frame, then you can be absolutely certain that your wife will fight you tooth and nail to prevent this. Expect the shit tests to escalate to never-before-seen epic-levels as she pokes and prods at this "new you," to see if you truly are taking your balls back out of her handbag. Or if you're just faking it.

- Before getting married, go see a divorce lawyer together and do not be guilt-tripped or shamed by your LTR for doing this (that, in and of itself, is a major red flag). Invest the money needed for a one-hour consultation with a local divorce lawyer to find out how a divorce would pan out where you live. Just think, if a skydiving instructor informed you that, not only did your parachute only have a 50% chance, or less, of opening. But, that you would also immediately lose legal access to everything that you had worked hard for the minute you jumped (including access to your kids), would you still want to jump out of that plane?

Steve From Accounting's Field Report

I've had quite a few friends and acquaintances ask me if I'll "ever get married again." I've told them that I can't unsee what I've seen of how marriage and divorce *truly* works (now that I've gone all the way through it and come out the other end). I explain that it's also unlikely that I'll ever cohabitate with a woman again either - usually to many a raised eyebrow. Personally, I see no value in marriage anymore (outside of raising a family with a woman that's 100% within your frame).

I simply state that I value my own space more than I value living with someone else and it'll certainly never be entertained while I make sure my kids get to grow up to become incredible adults.

I ignored an ungodly amount of the red flags noted in this book and many of the key areas noted in this chapter alone. My one saving grace was that I married someone who made *far* more than me financially and she was the one who ultimately lost almost 40% of her gold-plated defined benefits pension and a sizable chunk of money from the equity in the joint home in our divorce (along with a legally-binding court-order forcing her to pay the **vast** majority of the private school fees for our kids).

However, my divorce cost me the best part of £55k ($70k), it also took two painstakingly long years and it took a kick-ass female barrister (and **female** judge, who 100% had *my* back - for real) to get it squared away once-and-for-all. However, the UK's Family Courts don't recognize 50/50 custody like many states in the US do (it's not even a *thing* here), so I had to make a choice of spending a shitload more money on my credit cards (that I no longer had the limits for) to step into a legal framework that's against me from the off - or get creative.

I'll never forget a statement I read in a r/Divorce thread on Reddit a couple of years ago. In it, the poster mentioned how his solicitor gave him the following piece of advice:

 "Be careful how much time and money you spend, just to watch your kids sleep."
    - *Unknown (but smart) solicitor*

You see, child support (at least here in the UK) is dictated by how many overnights a child had with the "Non-Resident Parent" (or, NRP). You can also be on the hook here until the child leaves higher education (potentially up to when they turn **20**).

However, instead of stepping into a court system that isn't even *remotely* friendly towards fathers (no matter *how* much of an involved parent you are), and spending upwards of £20k+

on the risk of getting legally fucked over for years to come, I chose to fight for as much **quality time** as I could with my kids. Time where they were awake, so I could connect with them and strengthen my bond with them. You can't do that while they're sleeping.

So, instead of fighting for more nights, I fought to continue to take them to school everyday (like I always have done), pick them up from school most days, give them dinner and a bath at my home, and then their mum comes and collects them in the evening to take them just a minute's drive away from where I now live.

Sure, my ex-wife may get a few hundred extra pounds a month extra from me in child support, but I still have equal parenting rights (vital), half of the holidays, and every-other weekend (along with seeing and hugging my kids every school day), and a few extra nights when my ex-wife wants to go do something.

I can always make more money; I can't make any more quality time with my kids.

It's also important to note that this arrangement also gives me most evenings free to either work on growing my business, do some cool hobbies, or go on dates. Once my kids turn 13, *then* I can take a closer look at things again as certain aspects change legally.

If you're going to be crazy enough to marry someone, then FFS, do a load of due diligence as you could royally screw up your life if you don't. I've seen *far* too many horror stories of father's being physically dragged from their homes by false Domestic Violence (DV) charges in the US, or being screwed over six-ways-from-Sunday by their legal system.

I consider myself *verrrrry* lucky (when compared to a lot of these other fathers in the West) and I will **never** forget Rich reminding me of this perspective in one of our 1-1 calls. He simply told me that there's **plenty** of fathers out there that would jump into your shoes *in a heartbeat* if given the chance.

So far, I've got an *exceptionally* strong bond with both of my kids. My daughter still holds my hands as I walk her to her school gate (well, at least for now), and my son gives me huge, heartfelt hugs as I drop him off to his school. Unfortunately, *nowhere near* enough men are that lucky, and there's no guarantee that you will be either if you marry the wrong woman and have kids with her.

---

1. Review of General Psychology © 2009 American Psychological Association 2009, Vol. 13, No. 1, 59–65
2. US D.H.H.S. news release, March 26, 1999
3. Fulton County Georgia jail populations, Texas Department of Corrections, 1992
4. Centers for Disease Control
5. U.S. Department of Health and Human Services press release, Friday, March 26, 1999
6. US Dept. Of Health/Census

STEVE'S VERDICT - RICH'S ADVICE WORKS

Hopefully I've given you a good idea of just *how* effective Rich's advice can be when you do the work and do everything you can to live your best life possible (versus wallowing in self-pity and victimhood). Once again, I'm definitely no GigaChad, I'm certainly not 6ft tall, I don't have a full head of hair, I'm not a millionaire (but I'm damn well working on that), and I've still got a metric *fuckton* of work left to do.

However, the results I've got so far - from the moment I took my own balls back in 2018, up until now (August 2023), have truly been ***life-changing***.

Back in 2014 I was earning shit money and I was a fucking shell of a "man" (more man-child than anything). Now? I'm **genuinely** living my best life to-date (and it's only getting better). I've got two incredible young children who are my reason for pushing harder everyday. I want to set the best examples for my kids that I possibly can, whilst instilling in them the concepts I've learned over the last 9+ years.

My income is now firmly *well* into the $100k category (between my career and my - quickly expanding - business), I'm now wearing fitted clothes (tailored by a local lady who worked for some top-tier shirt companies in the UK) on my strongest physique to-date, and I have **zero** scarcity mindset in anything in life now.

It's important to note that I haven't done *everything* from this book to the letter. However, I *have* applied Rich's advice in a way that is congruent with **my** particular life goals and personality, and I've found that it's accelerated my personal growth in a manner that I *truly* never thought was possible.

Granted, I still have to deal with a pain-in-the-ass high-conflict ex-wife (who just *loves* to weaponize our kids when it suits her). However, the B.S. I must endure from my ex-wife is merely the cost of doing business and it's the price I've had to learn to pay to have the two most incredible humans in the world *along* with a life-changing amount of trauma that forced me to take a look at myself, and then find the ways to change my life for the better.

How can I be anything *other* than grateful for that?

I've also experienced what **genuine** burning desire from women looks (and feels like) and it's in a *whole different league* to what my relationships of the past have been. Are any of them "the one"? No (because "the one" doesn't exist).

Finally, I'd like to personally thank Rich for the opportunity to edit his book as it provided a timely, and poignant, reminder of the value and importance of owning my own shit as a man as I was navigating my shitty divorce. His 1-1 calls offered real insights and value and I've already connected in-person with a few amazing brothers from the 1% community on an international basis (with several more meet-ups planned this year).

FFS gentlemen, go do the work and build the life *you* want to live. I **promise** you that you absolutely *can* do it. By all means, make mistakes along the way (it's an essential part of the process after all), make sure you learn from them, and then continue to grow and update your belief system. I look forward to seeing you in the 1% community, sharing with the rest of us there how you too changed your whole life around for the better.

Now go fucking smash it!

Steve From Accounting

17

IN CONCLUSION

So, there you have it. Several of society's most comforting lies are crushed by a series of cold, hard, and uncomfortable truths. Allowing your eyes to open up to these truths is the basis of the ultimate playbook to understanding how to get better results in life and with women. Ultimately, transforming you into that Unplugged Alpha you want to be.

This book is just a no-bullshit introduction to the harsh realities that men around the world face today. There's much more to unpack, which I may release in a future book. The red flag chapter for example, could contain significantly more red flags. But, for the sake of simplicity, I had to distill that chapter down to the basics.

Throughout this book, I've referenced several other books that I strongly suggest you read. Consider those books next if you'd like to dive even deeper into the rabbit hole of becoming more alpha and masculine.

When you take the Red Pill, it's like being parched and then taking your first drink from a firehose. You're thirsty for the information, but the sheer volume of information comes at you with a shocking intensity and speed.

With that in mind, I'd suggest reading this book a few times over. Especially if my cold, hard, truth bombs make that Beta inside you feel deeply uncomfortable.

If you are new to my work, I invite you to browse my YouTube channels called 'entrepreneurs in cars' and 'the unplugged alpha' which is a podcast I run Monday nights at 8pm EST, to build upon the ideas in this book. I've uploaded almost 1,500 free videos for you to watch and learn from. They're the perfect complement to the information and life lessons contained within this book.

Similarly, if you are looking to connect with like-minded men from around the world that are actively working on becoming a top 1% man, then consider joining my private men's community. I offer my members many exclusive benefits, including discounted 1-on-1 coaching with me. Continue your journey by watching the introduction video here: http://entrepreneursincars.com/community/

My personal website is www.richcooper.ca

Finally, it's essential to remember: The point of unplugging from the comforting lies you've been told by society isn't to hate women, or to even leave a nasty taste in your mouth. It's about understanding, and then *fully* accepting the realities of living life as a strong, driven, and masculine man. Which includes the requirement of being *truly* at peace with women and not hating them for what they can never be to you.

Peace,
Rich Cooper

GLOSSARY

Oneitis

An unhealthy attachment to one woman where a man desperately pines for her love, attention, and intimacy. The woman in question often couldn't care less about his existence. Men who get "oneitis" often subscribe to the notion of her being his "one true love", only to see her move on to another man. All while he suffers and sulks in misery hoping she will, one day, return.

Spinning plates

This is a term used to describe simultaneously dating multiple women in a non-monogamous fashion (aka: casual dating). It's a tactic that's often used by men who are disinterested in a conventional monogamous relationship. Or, by someone who knows he is prone to developing "oneitis," or likes vetting women for an LTR/wife by providing contrast - allowing the cream to rise to the top.

It's important to note that you *never* overtly state you are spinning plates. You just do it, and let your actions signal, by the lack of your availability, that you are spinning plates. Women are, unknowingly by nature, master plate spinners, and often date multiple men at once. Unless, of course, they feel that they've found their best hypergamous option.

SMV (Sexual Marketplace Value)

An individual's own value on the sexual marketplace. For example, your physique, style, game, frame, confidence levels, etc. all have a "value" to women. The more you chase excellence, the higher your SMV naturally becomes as you optimize every area of your life.

"The Wall"

There comes a time in a woman's life when she can no longer really compete on the sexual marketplace with younger, more virile women, and they have therefore "hit the wall." Women are beauty objects to men and her SMV peak is around 23-years old. After that, she is steadily on the decline.

While you'll never openly hear a woman admitting to the existence of "the wall", if you ever hear 30+ divorced women talk between each other, they'll talk about giving their "best years" and often ask their friends "who wants a 30-year old with two kids in tow?" Like it – or not – they *know* that their prime asset is on a *very* steady decline.

Women can accelerate her impact with the wall with bad lifestyle habits like smoking, drinking, drugs, or by becoming a single mother. Conversely, a woman can also slightly push back hitting the wall by mastering self-care. Either way, a hot 23-year-old will *always* be more attractive to high value men than a relatively hot 43-year-old (as the latter now has a lower SMV).

Men also hit the wall, but a man's decline doesn't begin until he's in his mid-late thirties (or *much* later if he's a high value man). For more, search: "What is (SMV) Sexual Marketplace Value & The Wall" on my YouTube channel.

Soft Next

A "soft next" is where you completely cut contact with a girl for a few days immediately after she displays any really bad behavior (may be longer, depending on how often you see her, or how bad the behavior was). You do not respond to her texts, calls, or attempts to see you. It's essentially short-term ghosting.

The soft next works because it anchors negative consequences/emotions to bad behavior. For women, attention is the coin of the realm, and removing your attention powerfully resets your frame as the dominate frame in the relationship.

However, it's *critical* that, at the end of the soft next, you simply continue the relationship normal and act as if nothing had ever happened. If she took the hint that you're more than prepared to hold your boundaries firm, she'll be more than happy to meet up with you again.

Shit Test

Also known as a competency test, women often shit test men to see if they are their best option (aka: hypergamy). It can be a question, or a behavior she exhibits to test the frame of the relationship, and watches as to how he responds.

An example of a shit test might be: "Hold my purse for me." But, what she's *really* testing you for, is to see if you are a good little compliant beta male that will do as he's told, and stand there holding her purse like an obedient little puppy.

A simple "No, I don't carry female accessories" with a slight sneer would suffice. Hypergamy means that women will *always* shit test men (whether that's consciously or subconsciously), but the frequency and severity of the tests will reduce to almost zero when she is fully in your frame.

Hypergamy

Women's primary sexual strategy for millions of years has been to form a sexual relationship with a superior man on the socio-economic scale. It's often said that hypergamy doesn't seek its own level. Rather, hypergamy always seeks *better* than itself.

This is an evolved survival technique for her and her children to always find the best male she can secure for provisioning and protection. When a woman leaves a man, for another that she deems to be of higher value, it's because of hypergamy (also sometimes referred to as "monkey branching").

Many men are furious at women for being hypergamous. However, there's no value in being angry at a woman for wanting the best she believes, rightly or wrongly, that she can get. Understand hypergamy and make it work *for* you. To dive deeper into hypergamy, search for: "what is hypergamy" on my YouTube channel.

AFTERWORD

I met Rich Cooper in 2016. I'm loathed to call it a meeting, since it seems like no one really meets anyone face-to-face these days. At least not in the online spheres. Rich hit me up via email and asked me to come on his YouTube podcast, Entrepreneurs in Cars, for an interview.

Hell, I didn't even show my face until 2017, but something about Rich's email struck me as raw honesty. I've always been very hesitant to talk with guys who I got a grifter vibe from, but I didn't get that from Rich. He was sincere in his appreciation for what I put in 'The Rational Male' in a way that made me think: *"Alright, I'll take an hour to talk with him."*

I'm glad I did. Since that first meeting, Richard Cooper has become a good friend, business associate, and a mind with whom I could bounce ideas off of. He's a man who's experienced a lot, has the stripes to prove it, but more so, he was honest in his assessments.

Rich is a guy I would hang out with had I initially met him *in real life*. I didn't meet Rich face-to-face until September 2017. But, when I did, we just talked like old friends. No pretense, no fawning admiration, just two men who related like men.

I think he may have mentioned something about my work saving his life, but beyond that, we became fast friends. Since then, Rich and I have worked on collaborations both good and *unwise*. Even through the worst of decisions, Rich has proven a good and balanced friend. But, at the risk of glossing him up too much, Rich is *honest* with himself — and this is the prime requisite of a true *author*.

So, it is with that where I will leave Richard Cooper, and you the reader, with a note of advice from one *author* to another: Stay honest with yourself and read this book with the intent of internalizing the ideas contained within.

— *Rollo Tomassi, November 2020*

CURATED EIC YOUTUBE PLAYLISTS
WITH SCANNABLE QR CODES

Become a Better Man

Self Care

Entrepreneurial Tips

Money Advice

Dating Advice

Divorce Advice

Marriage

Parenting

TUA Podcast

Before the Trainwreck

Printed in Great Britain
by Amazon